How To
Create and Deliver
A Dynamic Presentation

DOUG MALOUF

ASTD **American Society for Training & Development**

Delivering Performance in a Changing World
1640 King Street
Box 1443
Alexandria, VA 22313-2043
PH 703.683.8100, FX 703.683.8103
www.astd.org

ACKNOWLEDGEMENTS

The author would like to thank the following for their invaluable assistance in co-ordinating this book:
Sue Quinn
Larry Lucas—Senior Consultant with I.T.A.T.E.
Edward E. Scannell—Author and Lecturer
Decker Communications Inc., U.S.A.

HOW TO CREATE AND DELIVER
A DYNAMIC PRESENTATION
First published in Australasia in 1988 by
Simon & Schuster Australia
7 Grosvenor Place, Brookvale NSW 2100

Reprinted 1992 by
Dougmal Training Systems

First published in United States in 1993 by
the American Society for Training and Development.

Designed by Susan Kinealy
Illustrations by Alan Stomann

HOW TO
CREATE AND DELIVER
A DYNAMIC PRESENTATION

CONTENTS

FOREWORD

Audiences "down under" have had the pleasure of listening to—and learning from—Doug Malouf for a number of years. Having known and worked with Doug both here in the states as well as in Australia, I can personally attest to his lively, informative, and enjoyable sessions. He is an active member of ASTD, the Australian Institute of Training and Development, and the National Speakers Association.

He has been a frequent speaker at HRD events, and his programs for ASTD and NSA are always top rated. Readers of this book will quickly see that his writing style is as animated as are his programs.

How To Create and Deliver A Dynamic Presentation is aptly named, and it truly delivers as promised. You will find dozens of practical hints and presentation techniques you can use in your next session.

Ask any experienced trainer or speaker the three most important parts of any presentation, and they will likely respond, preparation, preparation, and preparation! Follow the pragmatic advice and principles offered in this book, and you'll be guaranteed a dynamic presentation.

Veteran HRD personnel and professional speakers will also agree that careful preparation may not totally eliminate those butterflies, but it will certainly get them flying in formation! Enjoy that flight!

EDWARD E. SCANNELL, CMP, CSP
PAST PRESIDENT, ASTD, NSA

Ladies and gentlemen ...your undivided attention please!

INTRODUCTION

There are three certainties in life:
- death,
- taxes, and
- having to get up and speak in front of others

A recent study asked 10,000 people to mark these three certainties from most to least feared: 32 percent put "public speaking" at the top of the list. That is, one-third of the people would rather die than speak.

All public performers — actors, opera singers, comedians — feel nervous tension just before they go on. You never lose that sensation — the tightening in the stomach and the quickening of the breath and pulse. I *still* get it — after 15 years and hundreds and hundreds of presentations.

The secret is to face that fear—and turn it to your advantage. There's a fine line between anxiety and excitement. Practice and skill will develop in you the ability to *control that fear* and get on with the show.

It takes time to develop these skills, or any skills. I'm sitting in front of the word processor now, feeling not very confident with this new machine that has pride of place in the office. Bit by bit I'm getting better. A few weeks ago I felt so intimidated that I wouldn't even look at the thing. Now I can play away on it happily for hours. I've moved from the "unwilling and unable" stage towards the "willing (although not-so-able...yet)" stage.

And it's the same with getting up in front of an audience. It takes perseverance.

Those of you who have seen my first book, *Confidence Through Public Speaking* will have come across this idea already. So why this second book? What's the difference between public speaking and presenting? The following table shows the main differences:

	TYPE OF SPEECH	ADVANTAGES	DISADVANTAGES
PUBLIC SPEAKING	• social • political • competitive • entertaining	• quick and easy to prepare and deliver	• passive learning only • low retention rate
PRESENTING	• promotional • motivational • training	• active learning • high retention rate	• preparation time • needs equipment

A public speech *simply tells*. It is a "talking head exercise." *You* are the only visual and the length of the speech will probably be up to 20 or 30 minutes.

A presentation *shows*, *demonstrates*, and *involves*. As David Yagos, an old associate of mine, said: "Why tell them...when you can show them!"

WHO WOULD BE LIKELY TO GIVE A PRESENTATION?

Anyone who has to persuade, instruct, or "sell" ideas may need to give a presentation. That means *you*. Trainers, managers, lecturers, adult educators, and teachers are all required to give presentations—in short, *anyone* who wants to get a message across with *maximum impact*. This doesn't necessarily mean people in the business world—you might be presenting a proposal at your local school's PTA meeting, or reporting to your service club on some new proposal.

Whatever the occasion, a presentation involving *speaking*, *visual media*, and *participation* by the people attending will ensure maximum short-term and long-term impact.

A presentation could last half an hour or six hours. The longer it lasts, the more you'll have to involve visual media, activities, and variety of pace.

I'm a firm believer in the saying, "Practice makes perfect." The development of any new skill requires constant application.

If you have a message to get across, and you want the strongest possible impact, this book is designed for you. Make it work for you.

WHEN?
WHERE?
WHAT?
WHY?
WHO?
CONVENIENCE
SUITABILITY
MICROPHONE
AM I THE BEST
WILL I GET
DONUTS AND
A CUP OF
COFFEE
AFTERWARDS
WHAT
WIL
WIL

THE COMMUNICATIONS BOX

1

YOU'RE ON BEFORE YOU'RE ON

When communication consultant Dr. Edward Jones stated "You're on before you're on," he was emphasizing that your presentation starts from the moment you accept the job, not from the moment you first open your mouth to give your talk. Preparation is essential if you want your presentation to be a success.

CHECKLISTS

I find that the best way to prepare for a presentation is to use three checklists:

• **Two for myself** — the first assesses all the elements of the presentation and whether I should actually accept the invitation to speak, and the second assesses the equipment that I will need.

• **One for the organizer** — this helps to ensure that the organizer has everything ready at his or her end.

When I first consider taking on a new presentation I go through my "To speak or not to speak?" checklist (see page 11). This helps me evaluate whether I can do a top job.

CHECKLIST: *To speak or not to speak?*

Preparing a professional presentation is time-consuming. Save time by doing some preparation before you accept an invitation and consider the following:

The 5W's

When is the function?
Where is it?
What is it?
Why is it being held?
Who will be there?

Even a few checks in the "no" column will indicate that you should turn down the invitation, or at least find out more about what you are letting yourself in for.

		CONSIDER	YES	NO
WHEN IS IT?	Day .... Time .... Date .... Time given to me	Is it convenient, given other commitments? Is preparation time adequate? Is it appropriate?		
WHERE IS IT?	Location of venue .... Nature of venue .... Seating	Is it easy to get there? Is it suitable? Is it flexible? Adequate? Can I get what I need?		
WHAT IS IT?	Acoustics .... Resources available	Are microphone facilities available if required?		
WHY IS IT BEING HELD?	Type of function .... My role .... Purpose of function	Can I contribute? Am I the best person? Is it clear to the organizers? To me? To the audience?		
WHO WILL BE THERE?	How many people .... Background of audience .... VIPs expected	Is my expertise in the area greater than theirs? Am I confident I have something worthwhile to say?		

Once I've decided to go ahead and do the presentation I then go through my "Equipment that I'll need for my presentation" checklist.

CHECKLIST: *Equipment that I'll need for my presentation*

	YES	NO
Clock	☐	☐
Tape	☐	☐
Blank transparencies — clear	☐	☐
— blue	☐	☐
Pens for transparencies	☐	☐
Pen for presenter	☐	☐
Pens for students	☐	☐
Flipchart paper	☐	☐
Flipchart pens	☐	☐
Session transparencies	☐	☐
Key rings	☐	☐
Rulers	☐	☐
Books	☐	☐
One set of sample handouts	☐	☐
Whistle	☐	☐
Cassette/tapes/batteries	☐	☐
Radio amplifier	☐	☐
Extension cord	☐	☐
Overhead projector	☐	☐
Screen	☐	☐
Table	☐	☐
Microphone	☐	☐
Platform	☐	☐
Master copies of handouts	☐	☐
Folders	☐	☐

I then send a checklist to the organizer. The reason I do this is simple. Organizers of these functions are often too preoccupied with the big issues to be worried about their presenters, so when you arrive at the venue you will probably find that nothing is the way you want it.

A young man from a large company in Adelaide booked me for its state convention. Remembering my own words, I arrived early to check the equipment and layout, and guess what—he had delegated it to a lesser mortal and it hadn't been done. All the previous speakers used a lectern and a 6-foot stage, which meant they were about 20 feet from the audience. That wasn't for me. I like to speak from where I can be heard, so I arranged to meet the caretaker at 6 o'clock the next morning to set up the room in a way that would suit my style.

Now when I accept a booking I send out the "Checklist for the organizer."

CHECKLIST: *For the organizer*

To be sure we have a good seminar, would you ensure that we have the following equipment:

	I have organized:	
	YES	NO
— modern overhead projector/s and — extension cord/s.	☐	☐
— 2 ft 6 ins by 2 ft 6 ins table for the projector/s and resource material.	☐	☐
— 6 ft by 6 ft daylight screen/s. Please check the size as most screens are 4 ft by 3 ft.	☐	☐
— lapel FM radio microphone — no cords attached.	☐	☐
— platform/s—1 ft high, and 6 ft long by 4 ft wide. This platform enables me to maintain eye contact with the audience and allows excellent visibility for the overhead projector.	☐	☐
— pens/pencils.	☐	☐
— plain paper pads or note books.	☐	☐
— nametags.	☐	☐
— jugs of ice water and glasses.	☐	☐

Please arrange for room layout no. ___

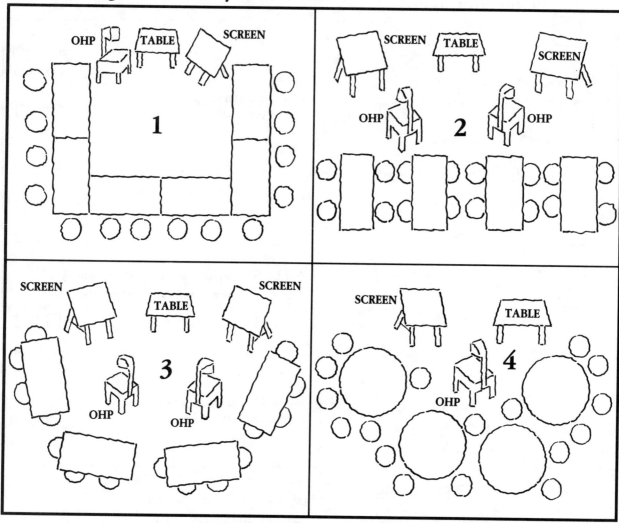

Even with a checklist for the organizer, things can still go wrong. Some people think an overhead projector is a 30 mm slide projector, a daylight screen is a wall, and a cordless FM microphone isn't possible. Unbelievable, yes, but if you're out on the trail as I am, you know it's true.

You are in control if you check it out first. When you're checking everything you need to think ahead of your audience. If you're going to say "You may care to write this down," then you need to think about pens and paper in your planning phase.

INSPECTING THE VENUE

If possible, you should inspect the venue before giving your presentation. Issues you need to consider include:

- Can you be seen by *everyone?*
- Can you be heard by *everyone?*
- Are there any distractions?
- Is the room comfortable and well ventilated?

Some years ago I was invited to address a conference of some 1500 people in Melbourne. Here is a plan showing the room:

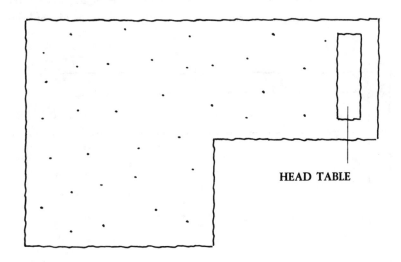

HEAD TABLE

What do you think *these people* will be doing while I am speaking in *this section?*

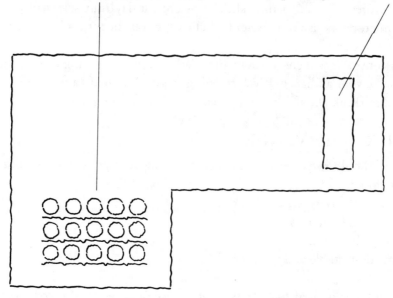

Answer: Making paper planes.

I arrived early and was told that I had to speak from the head table with the other speakers. No way! I arranged with the sound consultant to set up a microphone here:

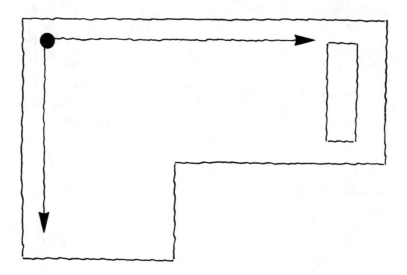

This meant I could at least try to maintain some eye contact—and it worked. When I was called on to speak I just left the head table and walked to the center point and did my thing. So don't be afraid of the organizer. You are the guest, not the servant.

REMEMBER:
- Your presentation begins from the moment you say, "Yes, I'll do the presentation for you."
- Start your preparation for your presentation at that moment and you'll maximize your chances of success.

ICEBREAKERS AND THE FIRST THREE MINUTES

For your presentation to have maximum impact your audience needs to be in a receptive frame of mind—right from the start. So, loosen up your audience. There is no point wasting time on the guts of your message when the audience is too uptight to receive it.

What you do before the presentation and during the first three minutes or so has a major effect on how your message will be received. Remember, first impressions count!

Some effective ways of making your audience more receptive include:

- being seen before the presentation
- making sure that the person who is going to introduce you to the audience uses a low-key but suggestive approach
- choosing an entertaining way to kick your presentation off—an icebreaker
- getting the audience involved—and keeping it moving.

BE SEEN BEFORE THE PRESENTATION

Many speakers don't agree with this—they prefer to hide in the back and make a dramatic entrance like Mae West. But my experience says be seen, shake a few hands, and thank them for coming.

I ask the organizer to provide name tags (the self-adhesive type) and so I introduce myself to the people as they arrive and help them with their name tags. It's a great icebreaker and lets people know you're human and that the day will be fun.

WRITE YOUR OWN INTRODUCTION

I was fortunate enough to be at the 1986 American Society for Training and Development Conference and hear Dr. Ken Blanchard, author of *The One Minute Manager* and one of the greats in the presentation world. I was excited about the prospect and expected a really dynamic session. But as the introducer started I was surprised at how low-key it was. I thought the introducer was underselling this outstanding personality.

When Dr. Blanchard walked to the center, he thanked the introducer and said that he'd had trouble with the introduction, so he always asked his mother to write it for him. With that sort of line it's no wonder that he had the audience in the palm of his hand within one minute.

Now I didn't get the chance to ask him if he really wrote the introduction or not. The point is that it's much better to be *undersold* at introduction time, and then to *overdeliver*, than to be *oversold* and then to *underdeliver*. Most professional speakers insist that the introducer sticks closely to a prepared script.

So, write your own introduction and insist that the introducer keep closely to it.

THE FIRST THREE MINUTES

The countdown starts for you once the introduction has finished. Here is the routine I follow to help me cope with getting started:

- Stay seated. Count to five. Walk to the position slowly. Don't jump up and get into it too quickly—you need this time to settle the nerves down.
- Speak from where you can maintain good eye contact.
- Stand still for the first two minutes. Don't pace up and down or use exaggerated movements.
- Smile and look for friendly faces—they are always there. Usually they are speakers themselves and know what you're going through.

The Icebreaker

An icebreaker is an activity at the start of your session designed to:

- break through the barriers to communication
- loosen up your participants so they feel at ease
- prepare your participants for the message of your presentation.

Some audiences can be so stiff and unreceptive when you first see them that you'd think they were frozen in their seats. You have to chip away at those icy faces with some well-chosen strategy.

Humor is about the best way I know to break the ice. If you can get them to crack a smile or even have a little chuckle in the first couple of minutes, then the rest will fall into place.

The "character survey" (see page 21) never fails to get a strong response. First I show them the *top* part of the graphic and explain that the shape which they choose reveals what type of character they have. Then I uncover the graphic, shape by shape, and the audience undoubtedly believes this is a serious piece of psychoanalysis—until the final shape, the circle, is revealed...

CHARACTER SURVEY

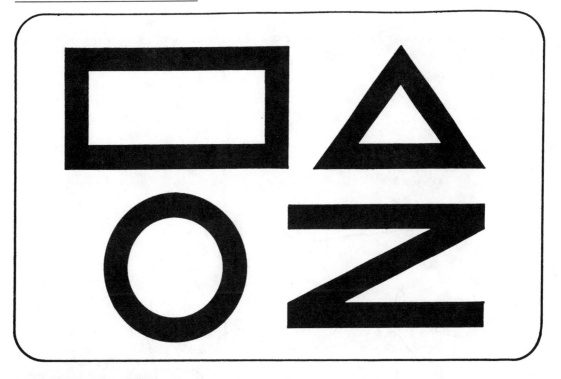

INTELLIGENT
Strong decision makers

LATERAL THINKERS
Prepared to look at all sides

CREATIVE
Strong imagination
Leaders

Preoccupied with
SEX and BOOZE

Reproduced from *Games Trainers Play*, by kind permission of the authors.

If the participants don't know each other before the workshop, I might use something like the "icebreaker card" to get them up and moving and familiar with their fellow participants (see page 23).

ICEBREAKER CARD

Each blank space identifies something about the people at this seminar. Seek out your fellow participants and if one of the listed items pertains to them, ask them to sign their names in the appropriate place on your card. (Even though more than one item may be relevant to any person, only one blank spot should be signed.)

Plays tennis	Is wearing red	Plays soccer	Apex member	Has grandchildren
___	___	___	___	___
Drives a sports car	Hates football	Loves football	Flies a plane	Plays piano
___	___	___	___	___
Drives 4WD	Has tropical fish	Eats hamburgers	Skis	Committee chairperson
___	___	___	___	___
Has red hair	Hates spinach	Has 2 children	Likes movies	Has attended National Conference
___	___	___	___	___
First time attendee	Speaks foreign language	Has brown eyes	Reads	Visited foreign country
___	___	___	___	___

Reproduced from *Games Trainers Play*, by kind permission of the authors.

A successful method I'm using at the moment, which lets participants know about me in a humorous way, and also involves them in the process of the session, is the "Who am I?" approach.

I start with a joke about my family name —Malouf. "I guess with a name like Malouf you may think I come from here."

I then stop speaking—turn on the overhead projector—and they see a color transparency of me on the back of a camel set against a background of pyramids in the middle of the desert. I then say, "But you're wrong—I come from Canowindra, Australia, 1,602 (population that is, not my age)."

My 'Who am I' icebreaker

Then I continue, "I was educated at St. Edwards Catholic School...By the way, how many Catholics are here today?"

I wait for a show of hands, and then add, "Well, I've got something very special for all the Catholics in the audience—key rings!"

My resource people, easily identified by their badges showing "Dougie's Little Helper," then quickly pass out key rings (which incidentally have the name of my company on them) to all those Catholics with their hands up. The audience loves it. They're involved and having fun.

When I reach the end of my "life story" I get them all up and at it with the direction, "Now meet a total stranger and tell him or her your own story in two minutes using the BIN formula."

What's the BIN formula?

- background
- interests
- name

Why do I do this? There are two reasons:
- The audience is involved in doing something in the first few minutes.
- The audience knows that this session will be fun—because I have shown them what to expect.

But what about the risks? Some people may think icebreakers such as these are childish. Some may even be offended by some of them. My experience, having worked with more than 3,000 people in one year, doesn't show that these doubts are justified. In fact, the comment I often get on my evaluation cards is: "I didn't get a key ring."

You might not feel comfortable with any of the techniques I've shown here. I vary the routine, but if I completely leave out such a routine, it always takes longer to make the participants feel relaxed. I've developed several structured icebreakers and now I never start a presentation without one of them. Once you're confident with your own, you can work them into any presentation you give.

Keep it moving

Evaluators of my presentations have commented on the speed with which I start my session.

"What's the big hurry — it's all I could do to keep up with you" was one of the comments.

Well maybe sometimes I overdo it a bit. But I prefer to be criticized for being too fast than for being too slow. There's nothing wrong with making the audience work also— after all, communication is meant to be a two-way process.

It doesn't really matter if some people don't catch *every* word at the start of your talk. (Obviously it's better if they do — and visuals help here.) What is important is that you're having *maximum impact* — you're drawing them into your world and grabbing their attention.

I move pretty fast right at the start of my session, catch their attention, and then relax the pace a little so they can stay with me.

Learn to make your presentation a moving picture — things to do — pictures to see— ideas to be shared.

REMEMBER:
- Loosen up your audience right from the start.
- Only *then* are you ready to hit them with the *big sell.*
- Always keep your presentation moving and MAKE IT FUN!

This is my apple tree approach... it gets to the core of all problems with communications!

3

THE APPLE TREE APPROACH

If there is one thing this book is about more than anything else it's *method*, the *way* in which you present yourself and your material.

Traditionally, public speakers and presenters have concentrated on *content*. We've all slept through the highly technical, painstakingly detailed speeches on everything under the sun. We've all been through school and some have even had to put up with higher education to realize how boring most teachers and lecturers are. The subject matter itself wasn't boring but the presentation was all chalk and talk, sit down and shut up, repeat after me.

There's absolutely no reason why you have to make those same mistakes when giving a presentation. The message is finally filtering through: *Learning must be fun.*

Learning must involve *variety*, *stimulation*, and *participation*. Learning must appeal to the *senses* as well as to the intellect.

We're all familiar with the old model of speech making: intro — body — conclusion. That model locked us in to an inflexible, outmoded way of structuring a speech which so often led to the overemphasis on content, to the detriment of method.

This is where the Apple Tree Approach to designing a presentation comes in. I was born and raised in the old school, but finally (being a slow learner) I came to understand why I kept finding myself talking to rooms full of sleeping people, or worse, dodging the paper planes.

In the Apple Tree Approach, the final presentation is the Apple Tree and the various elements which make it up are the apples.

The Apple Tree Approach offers a system of presentation design which I've refined over the years. The approach scraps the 8:1 formula (8 hours' preparation for a 1-hour speech) in favor of a 5:1 formula and rights the balance between method and content by building in:

- an appeal to the senses
- a variety of activities
- a chance for the audience to participate.

  The Apple Tree Approach is also:
- adaptable to any subject matter
- flexible in time
- most of all, simple to use.

Using the Apple Tree Approach means that there are five straightforward steps between you and a dynamic presentation:

STEP 1:
Give it a snappy title. _____

_____

STEP 2:
Reduce it to 5 "must know" statements.

1. _____
2. _____
3. _____
4. _____
5. _____

STEP 3:
Reduce your "must knows" to keywords.

STEP 4:
Build five minispeeches on each keyword using the ERS model.

E	Explain it.
R	Reinforce it.
S	Sell it.

STEP 5:
Picture it up!

How the Apple Tree Approach works

I will now go through an example step by step to demonstrate how the Apple Tree Approach works. The example I have chosen is a presentation on buying a computer for your business. Remember, the Apple Tree Approach assumes you know your content thoroughly!

Step 1: Give it a snappy title

First of all, work out what your theme or topic is and give it a catchy title. I've chosen "Beware the sharks—buying a business computer":

Step 1: Give it a snappy title. *"Beware the sharks—buying a business computer."*

Express the theme in positive words and keep it short and catchy.

Step 2: **Reduce it to five "must know" statements**

Step 2 involves selecting the five most important pieces of information which you want to pass on to your audience. Why five? George Miller, the American psychologist, in his famous article "The Magical Number 7 Plus or Minus 2," concluded that people (in the context of a presentation or public gathering) were able to remember only about seven pieces of information (plus or minus two). I have found through 15 years of public speaking that five is the upper limit.

How do you select these most important pieces of information? A useful technique is "brainstorming" — listing *all* the facts to do with the theme that spring to mind. When I brainstormed my theme, I came up with nine separate facts.

Then list the facts in order of importance, going from the "must knows" to the "should knows" to the "nice to knows." The top five facts on your list become the five pieces of information that the audience *must know.*

Write these five facts into the second box, reduce it to five "must know" statements. My five statements were:

Step 2: **Reduce it to 5 'must know' statements**, e.g.

1. You get what you pay for.

2. Prepare yourself and your staff for the new computer.

3. You are still going to be the one in control.

4. Make the most effective use of your computer.

5. Focus on its positive effects.

My explanations of these five "must knows" were:

1. *You get what you pay for*, so go for quality. A cheap unit will have only a few functions, break down quickly, and have no backup service.
2. *Prepare yourself and your staff for the new computer*. Organize in-house training and accept that you'll have to let go of the old system you've been using.
3. Decide right from the start that *you are still going to be the one in control*. Don t be a slave to a machine.
4. *Make the most effective use of your computer* by organizing its supplies and surrounding space efficiently, and by keeping it in good working order.
5. Once you've bought the computer, give it a fair chance by trying to *focus on its positive effects*. Don't badmouth the idea of working with a computer.

Step 3: **Reduce your "must knows" to keywords**

Keywording means condensing the essential message of your information into one easily remembered word or phrase. The keyword is the word which is the "key" into your subtopic. I reduced my "must knows" to these five sets of keywords:

1. Don't buy toys.
2. Gear up for installation.
3. Who's the boss?
4. Use it effectively.
5. Promote it.

These are then inserted in the box for Step 3.

Keywording helps you in two ways: it crystallizes your thinking and it cuts out the need for detailed scripting.

Keywording also benefits your audience by allowing them to see the core of your message at a glance.

People often say to me at my workshops, "Doug, your method is okay for straightforward subjects, but my material is much too technical and complicated to fit into the Apple Tree model. How can I reduce all my mass of information into five key words? It just wouldn't work."

I might have been excused for having the same thoughts when Apex handed me a two-inch thick document on children's leukemia and asked me to come up with the best way of publicizing the situation. There was a veritable encyclopedia of facts and figures, case studies, and strategies and I had to find a way to present it to the public.

The daughter of one of my close friends came to the rescue in the form of a story, which had been doing the rounds of her school that day. Please read the following story very carefully:

You are driving a bus that contains 50 people. The bus makes one stop and ten people get off, while three people get on. At the next stop seven people get off the bus, and two people get on. There are two more stops, at which four passengers get off each time. And three fares get on at one stop, and none at the other. At this point, the bus has to stop because of mechanical trouble. Some of the passengers are in a hurry and they decide to walk. So eight people get off the bus. When the mechanical trouble is taken care of, the bus goes to the last stop and the rest of the people get off.

She asked me to read it and then asked, "What was the name of the bus driver?" Of course, I didn't have a clue. There had been so much detail in the story that I'd forgotten the very first word, "You." I'd become so bogged down in the detail that I'd lost the main point.

This was the approach to the children's leukemia document—you'd lose your audience in the undergrowth if you tried to relate all the detail. Apex kept it simple, and came up with "Help a kid make it." That was the essential point—the key to the thing.

And that's my experience with presenting complicated subject matter. *Go for the heart of the matter* and leave the detail to a background handout if necessary.

Step 4: **Build five minispeeches on each keyword using the ERS model**
How do you structure your minispeeches? Try the ERS model:

- Explain it.
- Reinforce it.
- Sell it.

Explain it: Your keywords need explaining to your audience. Your explanation will be based on the material you wrote in the first "must know." As this is the opening of your minispeech, the explanation must be crystal clear and spoken with energy.

These were the notes I wrote next to "Explain it" in Step 4 under "Don't buy toys."

A cheap unit:
- has few functions
- breaks down quickly
- has poor backup service
- leads to dissatisfaction and frustration.
- You get what you pay for.

Reinforce it: In this part of your speech you bring in a number of reinforcers or motivational devices that arouse interest in the audience and help them to remember your information. Refer to the list of 11 reinforcers in Chapter 4 (page 50). Add your own to the list for more variety.

The three reinforcers I chose for "Don't buy toys" were *anecdote, demonstration, and facts and statistics.*

The *anecdote* was based on the experience of a business acquaintance of mine, Ed Johnson. He bought a cheap brand expecting the world—and got peanuts. What he ended up with was a glorified typewriter, which is okay if that's all you need. But he was after full filing and programming functions and was frustrated with the many limitations of his new machine. I'm not sure whether he threw his coffee mug at it, but by the second week it had stopped working. Hours on the phone trying to locate the computer company finally turned up a scruffy-looking repairman from the Emergency Breakdown Department. "The job's too big for me. You'll have to call in the Service Department," he said.

They eventually showed up and carted Ed's computer away. That was three months ago and he hasn't heard from them since. Now he resorts to hiring time on a computer on the other side of town.

So next to "reinforce it" I wrote, "Anecdote—Ed Johnson's cheap computer."

The *demonstration* I chose for "Don't buy toys" was an actual computer, but a good one from a well-recognized company with a nationwide distribution and service network. Not just the computer was on show, but also examples of the work it could do, with brochures and information.

I invited the audience to get hands-on experience and explained the computer's features and benefits.

The third reinforcer was *facts and statistics.* When I was first looking for a business computer one of the salesmen claimed that the best unit for me had a capacity of 30 megabytes, or 30 mb, as he put it.

"And what does that mean?" asked I, computer illiterate at the time (things haven't changed much).

"Well there are eight bits to a byte and..."

"Stop! Speak English, not computerese," I said.

"All right, that's equivalent to all the information in three *Encyclopedia Britannicas,*" he explained.

Now that *did* mean something to me. I finally knew what he was talking about. I wrote down "30 megabytes" as my third reinforcer.

Sell it: As a presenter you are a salesperson. You want your audience to "buy" your "product."

Now, what you're selling might be a physical product, such as furniture, cars, or clothes. But more likely you'll be selling an idea, information, a way of thinking or acting. Perhaps you're trying to sell the benefits to your staff of a new method of organizing leave for annual holidays, or persuade them to accept that smoking in the office is unfair to non-smokers.

Whether it's physical or non-physical, you're still selling. You want your audience to accept and act on your message. The more you can show what's in it for them, the more successful you'll be.

With my "Buying a business computer" presentation I wanted the audience to accept for their benefit five ways of thinking and acting before and after buying the computer.

To have most effect your selling statement must be short, straight to the point, and easily remembered. Think of your "sell it" as a telegram—the more words you use, the more you pay.

The one I chose for "Don't buy toys" was mostly a warning, but finishes with a positive action: "Don't do what Ed Johnson did—*toys will cost you money, so go for quality.*"

I say, "*If you can't sell it in 15 words—flush it!*"

So, to summarize, this is what I wrote in the box for Step 4 under "Don't buy toys."

Step 4: Build five minispeeches on each keyword using the ERS model.

Explain it: *A cheap unit*
- *has few functions*
- *breaks down quickly*
- *has poor backup service*
- *leads to dissatisfaction and frustration*
- *you get what you pay for.*

Reinforce it: *Anecdote—Ed Johnson's cheap computer*
Demonstration—computer and information
Facts and statistics—30 megabytes

Sell it: *"Don't do what Ed Johnson did—toys will cost you money, so go for quality."*

Step 5: **Picture it up!**

It's time for visuals—pictures, designs, sketches, symbols, cartoons—anything that gets the message across by appealing to the eye.

On the TV screen in the box for Step 5 you list the visual material you're going to use. Chapter 6, "Using the Visual Media" goes into this fully, so in this chapter I will just explain the illustrations I chose.

To support the Ed Johnson anecdote I selected a sketch showing poor old Ed next to his candle-powered computer, sweating it out and getting nowhere. This sketch visually reinforces the frustration and dissatisfaction caused by a poor quality computer. I wrote "Ed Johnson's candle-powered computer" in the TV screen.

The illustration *to support the demonstration of the good quality computer* was taken from a sales and information brochure put out by the maker of the computer on display. I wrote "Industry brochure" next in the TV screen.

The illustration *to dramatize the "30 megabytes" story* showed a cartoon figure (me) imagining the 30 savage bites of Jaws, complete with flashing teeth. I added "30 savage bites" to complete the list.

Illustrations 1 and 3 were on overheads only. Illustration 2 was on an overhead and a handout (as I wanted the audience to take that information away with them).

So my Step 5 box for "Don't buy toys" looked like this:

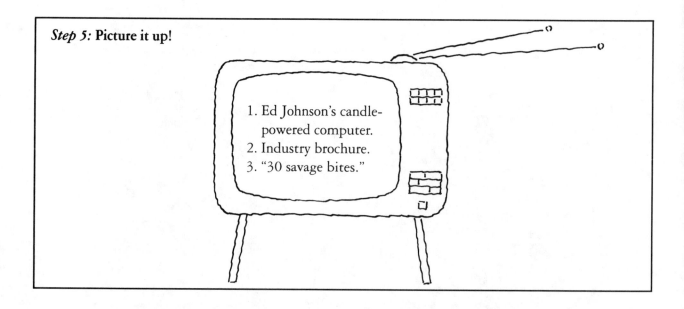

This completed the content and methods of presenting the content for the first minispeech. To complete the preparation for the rest of the presentation, I just followed the same pattern for the other four subtopics (expressed as keywords). I used the ERS model, then devised suitable illustrations to show the message.

Now I guess you are wondering whether this Apple Tree Approach really works. Certainly for me it does, and, as evidence that others are using it, reproduced below is the design for a seminar put together by a staff trainer who attended one of my seminars. Sue begins with a snappy title, "There's a smile on our dial," and her five "must knows" or keywords form the acronym SMILE. She then uses the ERS model to build the minispeeches and makes extensive use of visuals throughout.

There's A Smile On Our Dial

We shall use the acrostic SMILE for the program.

- S m i l e
- M a n n e r
- I n t e r e s t
- L i a i s o n
- E n t h u s i a s m

Two or three large posters of our company logo placed around room.

INTRODUCTION

5 mins.   Director of company welcomes delegates, confirms support for the program, and stresses importance of improving our skills, recapping on them, and ensuring we are better than our competitors.

15 mins.   BIN (background, interest, name). Delegates pair up and complete BIN handout on each other. Then, in groups of six, introduce each other to the rest of the group. Handout acrostic SMILE.

5 mins.   Sue introduces herself. Background—use of humorous caricature (transparency). Not long in the business, however give details of business history (resources in particular). Jogging and the dog. 80/20 rule—friendly people.

SMILE

Transparency for overhead projector showing our logo.

Explanation

5 mins.   Hand out logo stickers. Mention how often advertisements on TV now show people smiling. Transparencies of people smiling—six with a smile and six with a scowl. Anecdote about the person who has every reason not to smile because of tragic circumstances (husband invalid), but makes the effort and gives a smile and a joke to all those she contacts. She is well liked and referred to as a very happy person. Anecdote about when we were children—when we fell over our parents tried to make us laugh and the hurt went away. You can't stay unhappy if you are smiling.

Reinforce

10 mins.   Have you ever happened to glance at yourself in the mirror when you are angry or sad? Transparency of a bride—and same person before the wedding. Even unattractive people can look pretty handsome when they are happy. Have you ever seen an ugly bride?

Turn to your neighbor (partner) and with an angry expression say, "Isn't it a lovely day?" Now try it with a smile. Try to sound pleasant/happy with a scowl on your face—it's difficult, isn't it?

Turn your back on your partner. I'll blow the whistle every two minutes (you'll be distracted, but that's what happens sometimes when you are on the phone). Try to trick your partner. Can your partner guess your expression? Now cover your face except your eyes—try to trick your partner again. Are your partner's "eyes" smiling?

Sell

5 mins.   Video — *Who's on First?* Bud Abbott/Lou Costello.

5 mins.   Practice smiling *every* time you answer the phone; pick up the phone on the second or third ring. Get your mind into gear and then your face into action.

Next time you are sad, angry, or frustrated, make yourself smile (preferably in front of a mirror)—it will make you feel better. Psychologists say that a hearty laugh does more to relieve stress and tension than any drugs available. I *promise* you that if you practice smiling more, not only your boss will be pleased with you, but all those around you. More important, *you* will feel better.

MANNER
Explain

5 mins. What do people think of us? — anecdote about people believing I am a snob. How do we portray our own image? Do we really care about ourselves? If we don't like ourselves, who else will? If we look good, we feel good. No excuse for being untidily dressed these days — hair to be neat and well groomed.

20 mins. Divide into groups of six. Spend five minutes writing out 10 pet hates that occur in telephone situations. Each group presents its list in front of the audience. Sue writes down lists on whiteboard.

Open discussion on problems — brainstorm on possible solutions.

Reinforce

5 mins. Hand out the don'ts for telephone response; e.g., "Hold on," "He's in a meeting." Give alternatives.

20 mins. Group situation. Using telephones, simulate a very busy situation. Give a set script to delegates (for the callers). In role play, participant must handle four calls at one time. Evaluation. Take turns. Sue to give example first.

10 mins. Still in group. Each person is to say what is his or her first impression of the person sitting next to them. (Sue to give example.)

Were impressions correct? Were you happy with the impression you gave? Will there be things you want to change?

20 mins. Survey of taped phone calls (from our own company and competitors).

Open discussion on results.

Sell

2 mins. Do you want people to like you? Is it important to you?

10 mins. Coffee break.

INTEREST

Explanation

5 mins.   Communication, rapport with people, we can all do it with practice. Do we disregard children, do we speak too quickly to foreigners, are we impatient with the elderly? Aura — first impressions. Eye contact. Distractions — get back to customers quickly.

Reinforce

5 mins.   Story about service department follow-up. How to cope with an angry client. (Don't tolerate too much rudeness from them — especially bad language. Excuse yourself politely and walk away. If on the phone (explain what to do). Let angry people talk themselves out. *Listen.* (Cartoon transparency of angry person.)

40 mins.   Customers are really everything. Presentation (video) by Paul Dunne — *The Seven Steps to Customer Satisfaction.*
           Participation (brainstorm).

Sell

5 mins.   Don't let other people make you negative. Misunderstandings — service and parts departments. Should talk together more.

15 mins.   Lecture (guest speaker) on communication.

LIAISON

Explanation

5 mins.   Listening — we have two ears and one mouth for a reason. Interchange. We hear what we want to hear. Examples: "Mr. Jones will call in tomorrow" (meaning he will phone in). Message given as "Mr. Jones will come into the office tomorrow." Think of more and get delegates to write their own interpretations.

10 mins.   Groups of six — six examples from each group on how it can happen.

Reinforce

10 mins.   Game of consequences in groups of six. (Make up their own 10-word sentences.)

5 mins.   Remember you *must write down* name of person calling and the phone number. Transcribe message word for word. Don't interpret.

15 mins.   Listen — video.

Sell

5 mins.   Must get it right first time — waste of time if not. Also costs money.

ENTHUSIASM

Explain

5 mins.   Tone of voice. The way we look. Do we like what we do? Know your product. Hone your skills regularly.

Reinforce

20 mins.   Role-play from scripts—to test enthusiasm.

5 mins.   Go out of your way to help people even though it is sometimes inconvenient for you. Example of switchboard operator recently. An experience with Sue. Try to imagine yourself in the other person's place. Remember, though, the world isn't "fair" — you should try to give more than you receive.

Sell

15 mins.   Lecture — personal motivation (get some movement into it).

10 mins.   Close.

Announce competition.
Complete self-addressed handouts.

Dinner and guest speaker

Handouts

1. BIN
2. self-promise form
3. list of don'ts and alternatives
4. the seven steps to customer satisfaction
5. the SMILE acrostic

Transparencies (for overhead projector)

1. happy/angry faces (six of three people)
2. there's a smile on our dial logo
3. angry customer
4. well-dressed/presented person and the opposite
5. caricature of Sue Quinn

Need to have

pens and pads
overhead projector
whiteboard
table
telephones
seven-steps posters
prizes for competition
microphone
whistle

Prepare

"pressure/stress" role-play scripts
enthusiasm role-play scripts
sentences for consequences game

Order

stick pins—logo
stickers—logo
posters—logo

REMEMBER:
Follow these five steps to presentation design:
1. title
2. "must knows"
3. keywords
4. ERS
5. visuals
and you will be able to plan your whole presentation in a surprisingly short time.

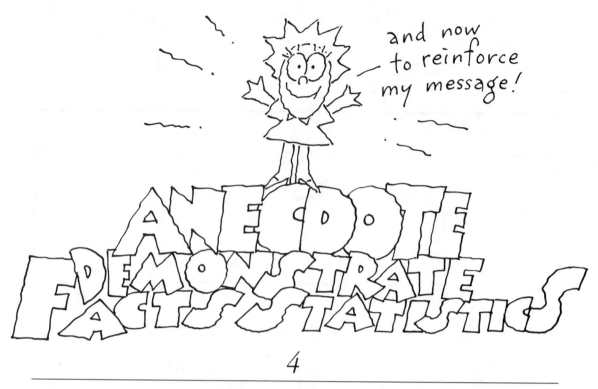

and now to reinforce my message!

4

REINFORCE! REINFORCE! REINFORCE!

Reinforcers are central to the successful use of the Apple Tree Approach. A reinforcer is any conceivable strategy for selling your message. Reinforcers:

- arouse interest
- get the message across
- help the audience *retain* the information.

In Chapter 3, I explained the Apple Tree Approach to presentation design and I listed three motivational devices which are successful in reinforcing the material:

- anecdote
- demonstration
- facts and statistics

In this chapter I want to look at 11 more ways of *packaging your product* to make it appealing to the audience and easily remembered:

- testimonials
- analogies
- case studies
- humor
- mnemonics
- games and quizzes
- repetition and restatement
- personal experiences
- participation
- examples and illustrations
- painting mental pictures

TESTIMONIALS

A testimonial is a statement made by another person and used by you to support your case. The bigger the name, the greater the impact, but it must be accurately reported and you must be able to support the statement. When you quote people in public it should be cleared by the author if possible.

Persistence is a topic I often deal with in my workshops and there is a testimonial to the power of persistence by Ray Kroc of McDonalds that I like to use:

Nothing in the world will
take the place of persistence:
talent will not; nothing is
more common than
unsuccessful men with talent.
Genius will not; unrewarded
genius is almost a proverb.
Education alone will not, for
the world is full of educated
derelicts. Persistence and
determination alone are
all powerful. Without
perseverance, living is
merely housekeeping.

RAY KROC

In my management workshops, I quote the words of inventor Thomas Edison, "I'll try anything, even Limberger cheese," to reinforce the need to be open to new ideas.

ANALOGIES

An analogy, or parallel situation, allows you to explain a certain point from a different angle. An analogy lets your audience understand your main point by seeing how it's similar to a more common experience.

One of the best analogies I've seen recently is the one used by the Australian National Heart Foundation promoting its anticholesterol campaign. The picture shows a person all dressed up in white overalls climbing into and journeying through a pipe that is supposed to represent blood flowing through the blood vessels. Now, on this journey all sorts of lumps appear in the pipe; we know they are cholesterol blocking up the blood vessels. Our hero starts to have more and more difficulty crawling along the pipe.

The analogy successfully gets the message across that too much cholesterol blocks the vessels.

You can lead into your analogy by saying, "Think of it this way..." and on you go. Complex subject matter can be made easily accessible with this technique.

CASE STUDIES

A case study is a working example that highlights a particular point or situation. A well-known Australian TV series, *Hypotheticals*, uses imaginary case studies to instruct viewers and demonstrate the workings of the law.

I came across another good example of a case study while I was attending a convention in St. Louis. The venue for the convention was the Sheraton St. Louis Hotel, which was undergoing extensive renovations during the peak convention time of year, so the hotel management was faced with a most undesirable situation. They realized that the only course of action was to turn the negative situation into a positive one.

What did they do? They made a game out of it: "In Search of the Renovator" (see page 54).

The game involved hotel patrons doing "detective work" — searching for clues that the renovators had left behind.

"Clues," such as dusty footprints, nails, or hammering noises, could be recorded by the hotel patron on a special sheet (see page 55).

Rewards, in the form of discounts on accommodation (see page 57), were received by patrons when they handed in their "Clues" sheets.

When I spoke to the hotel manager about the success of this strategy he explained that, far from being inconvenienced by the renovations, most hotel patrons had enjoyed taking part in the game.

As Dr. Edward Jones says, "Adults are just kids in big bodies."

The St. Louis Sheraton example is an excellent case study in how to turn a negative situation into a positive one.

IN SEARCH OF THE RENOVATOR

LOOK FOR THE "Clues"

Our $2.1 million dollar renovation here at the Sheraton St. Louis Hotel. All 615 guest rooms, our ballroom and guest room corridors are being renovated.

Once we're done, we'll not only be in the perfect location right next door to the Convention Centre and within a two-block walk to Laclede's Landing and St. Louis Centre, but we'll also be better than ever.

For your convenience we have taken great steps to hide all evidence of construction and workers while the renovation is happening...however you may suspect something is going on by the "CLUES" you find.

Renovators travel by secret passages, but sometimes they leave behind hints. If you discover that they didn't cover their tracks, give us a "CLUE" and we'll give you a reward!

We hope you will be as excited about our renovation as we are. Please enjoy your stay and your search for the renovator...and we hope you'll return to see how much better we've become.

Ⓢ

Sheraton St. Louis
AT CONVENTION PLAZA

"Clues"

The scene opened during check-in when you received this clue sheet.

You know the hotel is hiding renovators, and you don't have to be a detective from Scotland Yard to find the "CLUES".

It's elementary...they lie hidden throughout the hotel. Be cautious...check the boxes below if you're sure you saw the clue. Remember...it could be a trick!

Solve the mystery by turning this clue sheet into the front desk when you check-out. You will receive a reward for your deductions.

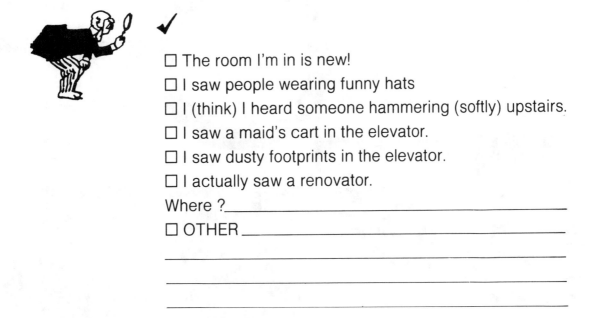

✓

☐ The room I'm in is new!

☐ I saw people wearing funny hats

☐ I (think) I heard someone hammering (softly) upstairs.

☐ I saw a maid's cart in the elevator.

☐ I saw dusty footprints in the elevator.

☐ I actually saw a renovator.

Where ?_____

☐ OTHER _____

_____

_____

_____

We think you're to be commended for your patience during our renovation...so we would like to give you 25% off your room rate* during your next stay with us.

We hope you weren't inconvenienced by the renovations and hope you enjoyed looking for the "CLUES".

It's no secret that we would like to have you back with us to enjoy the improvement of our renovation.

THANK YOU FOR THE "CLUE".

For reservations call (314) 231-5100 and ask for the special "CLUE" discount. Present this flyer at check-in.

HUMOR

The power of presenters is shown in the way they make humor work for them. Unfortunately, most presenters don't see themselves as humorists and so miss out on the many benefits of this powerful technique.

Humor has many benefits:

- Most of all, it makes people *feel good* to laugh.
- It relaxes and loosens up the audience, physically and psychologically.
- Laughing, smiling, and chuckling are all responses, so humor encourages participation. Only a dyed-in-the-wool cynic is immune to humor—most people can't stop themselves joining in for a good laugh.
- It unifies the audience. Everyone can see that everyone else is having fun, too.
- Humor adds variety to an otherwise serious talk, and adds a sense of anticipation—when's the next laugh coming?

There are seven rules of humor that I have distilled from my experience as a presenter:

1. It must fit you.
2. It must fit the audience.
3. It must fit the occasion.
4. It must be on you.
5. You must think it's funny.
6. It should come from experience.
7. It requires practice.

You need to be constantly on the lookout for material you can adapt for a presentation.

When giving a workshop on motivation, I couldn't resist using the one about the chicken: "The only living creature that produces dividends from a sitting position is a chicken...But they get plucked, stuffed, roasted, and eaten.

So unless you're into one of the above—*don't sit around.*"

Your own experience is probably the best place to find examples of humor. It also has the advantage of being directed at yourself—so no one gets offended.

I've always been a terrible speller and so I turn that into a joke by explaining, "If you can only spell a word one way, you're totally inflexible. If you see a word here today you don't understand—don't worry—it's only my spelling!"

MNEMONICS

Mnemonics are devices that aid the memory. By using a variety of mnemonic strategies, such as rhymes and acronyms, you will make it much easier for your audience to recall essential information.

Rhymes

A friend of mine has a three-year-old daughter who can't read or write yet but she knows her alphabet perfectly by chanting the "Alphabet Rhyme"over and over again:

A B C D E F G,

H I J K, L M N O P,

Q R S, T U V,

W, X, Y and Z.

Now I know my ABC,

Won't you come and play with me?

Whether you're a three-year-old singing along in the back of the car, a medical student remembering the names of nerve fibres coming from the brain, or a participant in one of my presentations, you'll find a simple rhyme will stay with you for years. (On a long drive the three-year-old's father wished the "Alphabet Rhyme" weren't so catchy!)

Acronyms

Acronyms, or words formed from the first letters of other words, are another way of aiding the memory. We're all familiar with such acronyms as "scuba" (self-contained underwater breathing apparatus) or START (Strategic Arms Reduction Treaty).

One of the senior trainers for a company I work with needed a catchy method of emphasizing to company employees the value of giving excellent service in their business. So he came up with the CARE program:

C	Customers
A	Are
R	Reason
E	Existence

His acronym was successful because the meaning of the word itself suggested the message contained in the acronym.

Whatever mnemonic you choose, keep it simple, clear, and closely related to the purpose — that way you'll help your participants retain your message.

GAMES AND QUIZZES

The main advantage of reinforcers in this category is that they are stimulating and fun. Games add variety to your program and encourage participation in an enjoyable activity by *all* of the audience. Although the activity itself is not reality, the learning that comes from it is certainly real.

A game I set up to impress on participants the power of asking the right question involves two or three people and a pack of playing cards. One person pulls a card from anywhere in the pack, keeping the front hidden from the other player.

The other player then has to find out what the card is by asking questions, such as, "Is it odd or even?" and "Is it black or red?" It can take about six or seven questions before you ask the right one.

To strengthen motivation I offer a reward, such as a key ring or ruler, for those who work out the answer with the minimum number of questions.

Quizzes also add variety to your program and act as very effective reinforcers. "The squares quiz" (see page 61) is an example of one I use in some of my workshops.

The Squares Quiz

How many squares can you see?

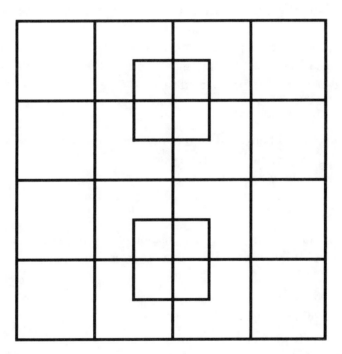

**Please record
your no.** ....

(See page 126 for answer.)

REPETITION AND RESTATEMENT

This is a strategy I follow all through my session — I don't save up all the repetition for just one moment in the program. I am constantly restating myself and restating my material. Some might say it's because I forget what I have said — sometimes they might be right. But mostly I repeat what I say so the *audience* doesn't forget what I say.

Too much repetition is likely to turn your audience off. Don't be so heavy-handed that they groan, "Oh, not that again!" Use repetition to *reinforce* your material and to show how much *emphasis* you place on certain aspects of your material. When you repeat a point in your presentation you're showing the audience that that point is more important than points you don't repeat. If they understand that you're repeating for emphasis and they accept your authority on that point, then it's likely they'll remember what you've said.

Restatement, or explaining a point in a different way, is a technique I use with more complicated or unusual material. By finding a number of ways of explaining a point, you maximize the chance of it being understood.

You'll find throughout this book, and even in my previous book, *Confidence Through Public Speaking*, that I keep coming back to certain points:

- Public speaking should be *fun* and *exciting*.
- *Method* or the *way* you present your material is of the utmost importance.
- Preparation is essential.

By this repetition, I'm showing you, the reader of my books, what *I* think is most important, and what *I* think you need to pay most attention to.

Do the same in your presentations:

- Tell them what you're going to tell them.
- Then tell them.
- Then tell them the same thing in a different way.
- And then tell them again if the point is that important.

PERSONAL EXPERIENCES

What's the one topic about which you're always an expert? *Yourself*, of course! That's why I often refer to my own experiences in my presentations — I know what I'm talking about.

You have a lifetime's experience filling your head, just itching to get out. Well, let it out and let your own experience work for you. Use it to reinforce the message of your presentation.

No one's going to challenge you because you know it best — it's *your* private storehouse of knowledge, which you are generous enough to share with others.

I keep a note of particular experiences and record interesting experiences as they happen. It doesn't matter if you can't see how you'll use the experience in a later presentation. It will become obvious to you when you need it.

A personal story can be adapted to a number of situations by emphasizing different aspects of the experience. You can use it effectively to reinforce a variety of points.

I often use the "Who am I?" approach as an icebreaker at the beginning of a presentation. Once I've given an overview of my teenage and adult life, I constantly dip back into it during the course of the presentation, highlighting various aspects of my own life story to back up the message I'm putting across.

My career in public speaking goes back a long way and there were many blunders and failures as well as a few successes along the way. By referring to some of the mistakes I made, I am able to focus on common mistakes that budding presenters often make, and, I hope, offer advice as to how to avoid them.

This "What went wrong" approach is particularly effective for me, not just because there are so many mistakes to choose from in my own career, but because it presents a nonthreatening and entertaining way for others to analyze their own experience.

So, keep a notebook of worthwhile material from your own life. Adapt it to the particular subject you're working on, and help others to change for the better by learning from your own experience.

Some presenters believe that you should never let the truth stand in the way of a good story. I'm not one of them. Apart from the absence of ethics in lying, there could always be someone in the audience who may dispute your story. This is why I like to speak from actual personal experience in my presentations — I *know* what I'm talking about and I can't be challenged on it.

PARTICIPATION

Participation is also a form of reinforcement — in fact, it's one of the most important reinforcers I use. It is so important that I have devoted a whole chapter to the topic (Chapter 5). Participation is a special technique. Unlike the other reinforcers, such as anecdotes, mnemonics, and humor, which are strategies centered on the *presenter*, participation mobilizes the participants to:

- use their *own* initiative
- make their *own* decisions
- develop their *own* effective working relationships.

While they're doing, they're learning. They're *practicing* and *testing* the message of your presentation. You will get the most out of participation if you see it as a reinforcer as well as a basic method of motivating and involving your participants.

EXAMPLES AND ILLUSTRATIONS

The effect of a statement you make will be much greater if you give an example from a well-known newspaper, magazine, or TV show. Have the article with you, hold it up when you refer to it, or have it on an overhead for all to see. The print media is full of examples and illustrations you can use to reinforce just about anything. Examples are effective because they allow your audience to relate to something currently happening in the world.

PAINTING MENTAL PICTURES

By using striking and imaginative language and visuals you will arouse the audience's interest and create strong mental pictures in their minds.

An exciting appeal to the five senses — seeing, hearing, smelling, tasting, touching — is much more likely to have a strong impact than bland and unimaginative language.

Does this present a vivid mental picture for you: "The boy ate the apple"?

Of course not — you can't hear it, taste it, or see it.

"The little boy's eyes lit up as he munched into the juicy red apple." In contrast to the first statement, this appeals to:

- taste — the apple is *juicy*
- hearing — he *munched*
- sight — his eyes *lit up*; the *red* apple

A distinct mental picture is created.

Always keep your senses open and note down examples that you come across. For example:

- the feel of a chilly, biting wind
- the bustle of shoppers pushing and shoving at a sale
- traffic and street noises
- the sharp, greasy smell of a hamburger stand

Later, build these "mental pictures" into your presentation, to reinforce, highlight, and arouse the imagination of your audience.

Unimaginative, colorless language and visuals have no part in your presentation — they're not worth the transparencies they're produced on.

Learn to paint *stimulating mental pictures* taken from your own experience and imagination, and you'll be using a powerful technique in communication.

REMEMBER:
- Always use reinforcers to help sell your message.
- Reinforcers, if used effectively, will help ensure that your audience *receives* and *retains* the message of your presentation.

5

PARTICIPATION

As I explained in Chapter 4, I consider participation a reinforcer of special importance. In fact, I consider participation *the* most important reinforcer — that's why I've devoted a whole chapter to it.

WHAT'S THE POINT OF ENCOURAGING AUDIENCE PARTICIPATION?

Some would say it's easier and more controllable if you just keep the audience sitting in their seats all day. After all, *you're* the expert they have paid to hear. All these games and groups and gadgets are beside the point, aren't they?

The answer depends on your understanding of how people learn. Do we learn best as passive recipients of information handed down to us by "the experts," who make all the decisions about when and how and with whom we learn? Or do we learn best through a process of interaction with specialists and peers, an *active* process involving a variety of methods and experiences?

I think it's undeniable that all learning involves some level of action by the learner. Even if you're asleep you can still learn — witness those memory and self-improvement courses that you play on your cassette player while you're asleep. In the morning you wake up and (depending on how much mental energy you've wasted on fantasies, dreams, astral travelling, etc.) you have partial recall of the material you "listened" to during the night. Your conscious mind was asleep, but your subconscious mind was even busier than usual, sorting and memorizing the taped material.

Or think of the now-banned subliminal advertising that "taught" TV viewers that "Whamo" brand laundry powder was the most desirable. The viewers were unaware of this hidden message because it zapped across the screen so quickly.

In both cases, sleep learning and subliminal advertising, learners were not consciously aware of what was going on. But at a deeper level, their subconscious minds were "learning" the message.

That's at one end of the scale.

At the other end there is learning that comes purely from doing, such as learning to catch a wave in the surf. You don't go to classes to be told about wave energy and formation, the buoyant capabilities of the human body, the influence of the wind, etc. You just get out there and do it because you enjoy it.

Most learning, though, falls in the middle of the spectrum. You can't learn physical or social skills by "listening" to a tape while you're asleep. Nor is trial and error the best way to learn all about your first computer. You read the instruction book (no easy job in some cases) and get others to show you, as well as getting lots of hands-on experience.

And so it should be in your presentations — a mix of listening, practicing, experimenting, and interacting. The participants *listen* to the expert, *learn* with their peers, and *discover* for themselves.

The researchers back up this approach with a wealth of findings in favor of active learning:

- It is one of the best methods of arousing and sustaining interest and attention.
- It allows the presenter to monitor learning and give guidance to learners while they are consolidating their learning.
- It allows learners to feel that they have some control over what they're doing and that they "own" the products of their work.
- Quieter, less assertive individuals are much more likely to participate in a small, nonthreatening group.
- The many and varied experiences and talents of group members are likely to lead to better decisions and a better understanding of those decisions.

SOME GROUND RULES FOR AUDIENCE PARTICIPATION

The activity must involve no risk for participants

This is the reason that role-plays often don't work in a presentation. The presenter creates a role and expects participants to get up in front of their peers and perform. The result? — awkwardness and embarrassment for the "performer" (and possibly for the audience as well).

Reverse the situation — *you* take the risks and *they* get the rewards. Get up and demonstrate exactly what you want. Show them that *you're* willing to step out on a limb. If anyone has to look the fool make sure it's *you*, the presenter.

They must be able to do the task

It can't be too complicated, too demanding, or in any way inappropriate to the abilities of the participants. You can't expect them to take part in an activity if they don't have the skills to do so. The activities can become more demanding as the day goes on and as they pick up skills and information. Similarly you must provide all the physical materials essential for the activity — pens, paper, transparencies, flipcharts, tables, overhead projectors, whatever.

The task must be clearly explained

You, the presenter, know exactly what you want the audience to do. The problem can be communicating that instruction to the audience in a way they can understand.

I remember a presentation I once gave to a group of advertising executives in Adelaide. Being ambitious myself, and assuming that this high-powered group, like me, would jump at a new challenge, I pitched the level of the explanation pretty high. It was obvious, I thought, what was expected. I was sure they would slip smoothly into their allotted roles.

Needless to say, we never did the role-play. I spent 40 desperate minutes trying to reexplain the activity to each of the small groups. Just as I finished explaining the requirements to the last group, it was time for the afternoon coffee break. By that time, I was more in need of refreshment than anyone else in the room.

It must be fun

If your activities are enjoyable for the participants, then benefits will result for you and them:

- They'll be happy to keep up their involvement in later activities. Group discussions, brainstorming sessions, role-plays, creating visuals — these are the types of activities they'll look forward to. Also, if your participants enjoyed *your* activities they're more likely to encourage others to be active back at the workplace, and even to use activities in their own presentations.
- The quality of the work they produce will be high. If members of the groups enjoy what they're doing, then they'll cooperate well, be willing to pool their previous experiences, and reach consensus easily.

METHODS OF INVOLVING LEARNERS

Listed below (pages 70-74) are 19 commonly used methods of presentation that lend themselves to varying degrees of participation. This is not a complete list of every technique possible. There may be others that you would like to add.

Putting participation in your presentation

	ADVANTAGES	**DISADVANTAGES**
Lecture: (verbal presentation by trainer)	• covers a lot of ground • large numbers • no interruptions • complete control over content	• passive learning • no questions/feedback • no use of trainee experience • can't progressively evaluate
Lecture/ discussion: (lecture followed by large group discussion)	As for **Lecture**, plus: • more motivation to listen • allows for questions/feedback • discussion can be controlled • can reinforce key points of lecture	• "comment hoggers" • selected participation • you don't know what non-contributors think
Modified lecture: (lecture mixed with student activity, e.g., individual or small-group work)	As for **Lecture/discussion**, plus: • trainees contribute from own experience • trainees learn from sharing experiences • trainees control more of content • greater participation	• trainer may have difficulty controlling discussion • may require additional help to facilitate • could run out of time if groups are too enthusiastic
Forum: (large gathering with participants expressing a range of ideas)	• immediacy • stimulating • many viewpoints • high involvement in a short time	• "comment hoggers" • difficult to control • may be superficial

	ADVANTAGES	DISADVANTAGES
Debate: (an organized argument between persons with opposing points of view)	• clear focus • shows opposing views • enhances listening skills • any number can view	• polarized (rigid) approach to issues • limited participation • depends on speakers' abilities • destructive rather than "idea building"
Group discussion: (structured exchange of ideas and knowledge)	• high participation • cross fertilization • allows for questions/feedback • fosters "idea building"	• some find threatening • "pooling of ignorance" • "comment hoggers" • deviation from subject
Buzz groups: (leaderless small groups with set mission and time limit)	• high involvement • nonthreatening • enjoyable • feedback to trainer • many ideas quickly	• possible lack of depth • can lose direction if not monitored
Brainstorming: (many ideas expressed without discussion or evaluation)	• breaks down inhibitions • creative and stimulating • quantity of ideas • nonthreatening • fun	• requires leadership of process • few quality ideas • little trainer input to content

	ADVANTAGES	**DISADVANTAGES**
Case study: (a situation or event to be analyzed)	• involvement and interaction • depth and detail • application of knowledge/skills • close to reality	• could produce "stereotyped" answers • requires time to analyze a report
Role-play: (activities that mimic real-life action/events)	• flexible for numbers of observers • efficient in changing attitudes and behavior • can be fun • provides confidence for real-life situations	• time-consuming • unpredictable • threatening to some • feedback must be handled well
Demonstration: ...of "how it should be done," normally step by step)	• understanding skills • promotes visual interest • step-by-step approach shown	• trainer must be a good "model" • large groups difficult • needs to be a simple process
Demonstration with practice: (demonstration followed by practice of participants)	As for **Demonstration**, plus: • performance can be corrected • high involvement • behavior change	• requires guidance • can be a negative experience • requires more time

	ADVANTAGES	DISADVANTAGES
Independent study: (trainer becomes an additional resource, in the trainee's pursuit of his or her goals)	• flexible • learner is responsible	• isolation — no group interaction • difficult to control • limited feedback/checks on progress • depends on trainee motivation
Films, videos, tapes: (resources)	• mass audience • popular with adults • flexible • entertaining	• equipment • preparation • can be passive • old or poor quality
Tutorial: (where each trainee is assigned a topic for presentation)	• individualized • varying styles of presentation • allows assessment of understanding of topic • learning trainees' responsibility	• difficult to control • may be boring
Self-discovery: (students discover attitudes and feelings)	• potential for attitude change • high involvement • fun • caters to various levels of learning	• difficult to control • "lazy" students • unforeseen circumstances • can lead to negative experiences

HOW TO CREATE AND DELIVER A DYNAMIC PRESENTATION

	ADVANTAGES	DISADVANTAGES
Exhibit: (a display of materials to aid learning)	• real • interesting • complements theory	• limiting for large groups • requires space
Field trip: (a planned tour)	• practical • experiential • firsthand observation • individual learning	• time and cost • identifying important items • logistics
Simulation / games: (experimental learning where students discover concepts and principles)	• increases understanding of principles • high involvement • fun	• "lazy" students • may be viewed as "childish"

WHATEVER METHOD YOU CHOOSE, KEEP IT MOVING

As was discussed in Chapter 2 on "Icebreakers and the First Three Minutes," I get the audience up and at it very early in the presentation — maybe introducing themselves to each other, carrying out a quick survey, or sorting themselves into groups in preparation for a later activity. Whatever the initial activity, the audience realizes right from the start that they will be involved in a variety of experiences, not just listening.

Everything I do in my presentations is designed to *catch* the audience's attention, and then *keep it*. It's so easy for them to slip off into their daydreams and fantasies. As the presenter, you have to work hard to keep their attention on you and your message.

Introduce an activity or flash up more visuals or vary the pace of your delivery. Stand on your head if you have to. Just keep them focused on the purpose of your session.

The way to do this is with a variety of stimuli and activities.

You can see why the word "audience" is inappropriate for this type of presentation-goer. An audience is a collection of people passively listening to or watching a performance. The presentations of today offer participants a feast of stimuli appealing equally to the eyes and ears, as well as offering a range of experiential involvement.

More and more, presentation-goers *expect* to be involved. You can't afford to ignore such an effective tool of communication and learning.

HOW TO PROMOTE PARTICIPATION

Your presentation occurs in what experts call a "learning environment." It is made up of the activities, venue, personalities, and abilities of the group, and the content and style of the presentation.

My observations, analysis, and experience all lead me to believe that learning flourishes in an active learning environment. As the presenter, you need to control all the elements of this situation so that an active response is encouraged. You want to bring about some sort of change in the minds and bodies of the people attending. You want to maximize your impact on the group, by manipulating all the elements in the learning environment.

Having worked with adults for over 10 years now, I've come to appreciate that the chances of effective learning are maximized when the learning environment is organized in certain ways. These are:

- where the "atmosphere" is relaxed and encouraging of the learner's efforts
- when the learners can have some effective control over their learning
- where active participation is encouraged
- where there is effective communication between learners and teacher.

My understanding of the principles of learning has helped me immensely in building a learning environment that allows the listener to participate — to respond to me.

If you have been a "talking head" for 20 minutes and then say, "Are there any questions?," nothing may happen.

The listeners don't want to ask what might be seen as a stupid question, so they don't ask any.

When I want to encourage a response, especially if it's early in the program, I say something like, "Let's hear *your* comments on what I've just said." Or, "Are there any questions, comments, or observations?"

Then, *I stop talking*, to show that I'm serious about hearing from the audience. Too often you hear a presenter ask, "Are there any questions?" and then keep talking. You have to train yourself to ask for the response, and then *shut up*.

If the audience is playing hard to get — no responses at all — I might slip in a bit of humor to liven things up.

Once the responses start coming — and they will if you show you sincerely want participation — then you must deal with those responses in a positive, encouraging way.

The TREES approach (page 77) is a strategy I've developed to deal effectively with audience response.

The T R E E S approach to handling audience response

Thank the respondent

> You can do this by:
> establishing eye contact
> using his or her name
> if possible

Restate the comment

> Restating the comment
> ensures that everyone
> can both hear and
> understand the
> comment.

Encourage the response

> Be positive.
> Deal with it.
> Hold it.

Ensure you've satisfied the respondent

> Ask, "Does that answer
> your question?"

Stay true to

> ...your material,
> your audience,
> yourself.

The big **U** = use the group as your resource!

Thank the respondent

You can do this by:
- establishing eye contact
- using his or her name if possible.

Restate the comment

Restating the comment ensures that everyone can both hear and understand the comment.

Encourage the response

Regardless of how negative the feedback from the audience, stay positive and calm.

As the presenter, you have two options. If the question concerns the issue at hand, answer it there and then. But if the question does not directly relate to the topic, you might want to leave it until later. The risk you run, though, if you defer answering it, is that you'll upset the questioner, or even the audience.

So you have to make a decision.

Let's say you *do* decide to put off answering it until later. How can you do this without turning the audience off?

One successful strategy is to use a "coming attraction page" on a flipchart easel. I first came across this technique with Dr. Edward Jones. He says to the questioner, "Would you mind if we hold that idea until later? I'll write it up on the `coming attraction page' to make sure we deal with it later."

I like this approach. The questioner feels that you have listened and, more important, seriously intend to deal with the question later.

Ensure you've satisfied the respondent

Auctioneers use the words: "Are you all done and finished?" meaning that's the end of that. So too with comments — try to tidy them up. Finish the issue there and then. Try not to leave any loose ends.

Check by asking: "Does that answer your question?" If not, why not? If it does, then move on to the next item of business.

Stay true

Stay true to your material and your values. You must respect your audience and yourself.

A recent experience of mine illustrates this point well. It was a consultancy job with about 30 people. Things were going well and I was speaking about the idea that lecturers and presenters need to let go of their material. A loud voice from the back row claimed that the speaker was the expert and should never let go. *He* was the expert as far as his staff was concerned and he knew best.

I immediately used the group as a resource. I said, "How does someone else feel about that statement?" A young man from the front row said, "I agree with you, Doug. A speaker should allow people in the audience to use their material instead of just sitting and listening." Our loud-mouthed friend from the back called out, "That's stupid!"

Now I had a decision to make — should I lose my cool and shout him down or should I respect my own and his opinion?

I replied, "This program is not a prescription, it is an idea exchange. If you elect to use any or none of these ideas, that's your option. But I would suggest you evaluate your own presentation, just to monitor how you are coming across to your group."

At this point, a second young man jumped up and said, "Doug, I know what they are saying."

"Tell us all," I said.

He replied, "They call him the motor mouth."

Well, the whole group exploded with laughter. The group itself had actually settled down the attack.

So don't ever be afraid of using your group as a resource. One of the benefits of doing this is that your audience usually comes up with a great deal of knowledge about *your* subject. The old saying: "Every adult is an expert" is true to an extent.

If you get a question you can't handle, say, "I'm not sure about that one. Perhaps someone in the audience could help us."

Don't use notes — use your audience instead!

In 1980 international consultant S. W. Brown arrived in town. I was his driver and guide during his stay. On the way to his first engagement he asked me what he should talk about. We decided on a topic and he immediately pulled out some bits of paper, jotted down some notes, and drew some stick figures.

"Are they your notes?" I asked in amazement.

"Hell no!" he said, "I'm just programming my mind."

He screwed up the page and threw it away.

Later that day he spoke for three hours — no notes, no nothing! But he had total audience involvement!

Day 3, and it was off to Melbourne. I was going to make a presentation, too — we had half a day each. We arrived at the airport. I had to find out how he did it without notes. So I said. "Where are your notes?"

He smiled, pointed to his brain, and said, "In here."

He looked at me and said, "What's that?" pointing to a large leather bag I was carrying. In this large bag were 10 billboards — 3 feet long and 1 1/2 feet tall — that I'd had made up by a professional sign painter. These hefty billboards were my revolutionary replacement for speakers' notes.

Mr. Brown looked, listened to me, and asked, "What happens if this bag gets lost in transit?"

I looked at him, swallowed, and said in a clear voice, "I don't speak."

He replied, "Learn to trust your memory — it always travels with you!"

One month later I jumped on a plane and attended his training school. That forced me to change and develop my AIMs — Audience Information Maps. Now I never use notes and never become lost — the audience holds my notes for me.

By maximizing the use of handouts and visuals and calling for total audience participation, I always know what I'm going to say and never have to hold notes. If I lose the thread for a moment, I just sidle up to one of the participants and glance at the last handout. *That* tells me what's going on.

What's the point in having all this in a chapter about participation?

Participation, like communication, is a two-way process. By insisting on active involvement from my participants I get two things:

• I establish an active learning environment.

• I ensure that they — the participants — keep me on the straight and narrow.

So by promoting participation you make it easier for yourself. A participating audience offers "information props" through its interaction, and so removes the need for notes.

REMEMBER:
• Participation *is the key technique* for promoting high-performance learning.
• If you have organized your presentation carefully, the participants will usually lead both you and themselves in the direction you want.

6

USING THE VISUAL MEDIA

Have you ever asked yourself why we use the word "see" in the expression "I see what you mean"? We could use "understand," but the word "see" has the special meaning here of "seeing with the mind" (not with the eyes).

This common use of language contains a vital message for the presenter or trainer: people learn through visual stimuli. Not exclusively, but the impact you make through visuals will be powerful.

The relative impact of the senses in the learning process are

- smell — 3 percent
- taste — 4 percent
- touch — 7 percent
- hearing — 11 percent
- sight — 75 percent

We know that it is twice as likely that presenters will achieve their goals if they use visuals effectively, and that a much higher rate of group consensus is reached when visuals are used. (See "Speakers without visuals" and "Speakers with visuals," page 82.)

Speakers without visuals

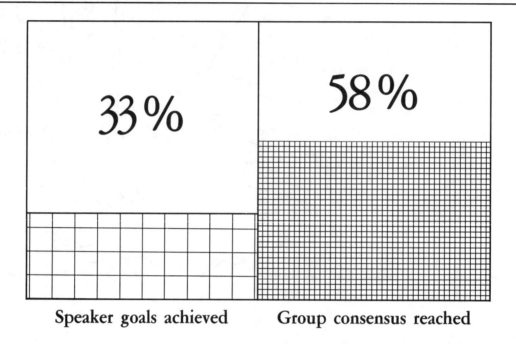

Speaker goals achieved   **Group consensus reached**

Speakers with visuals

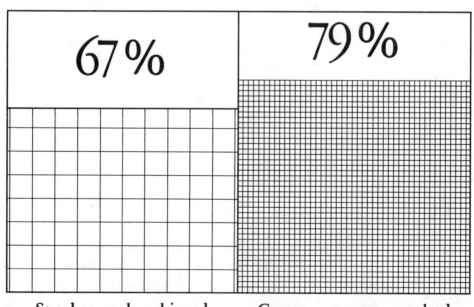

Speaker goals achieved   **Group consensus reached**

Decker Communications Report; Decker Communications Inc.
Cragmar Centre, Princes Highway, North Wollongong N.S.W., 2500 Australia

A decision on whether to use visuals in your presentation will depend partly on the length of your talk. The shorter the talk, the less need you will have to sustain the audience's interest and the less information you'll be able to get across. A presentation of more than one hour should include extensive use of visuals as well as encouraging active participation by the audience.

The advantages of using visuals in your presentation include:

- Pictures are processed by the mind with very little effort (unlike words that you hear).
- Pictures act as keys to the memory. Mental associations are quickly carried out through the stimulus of a picture. Sensory memory supports the short-term memory of verbal information.
- Pictures can easily illustrate tasks that words are not suited to.
- Vibrant visuals provide a common focus for the audience, and any loss of attention to the spoken word will be compensated for by the supporting visual material.
- Visuals allow the presenter to direct the attention of the audience toward his or her goals. Well-designed visuals are signposts — they allow the audience to see what direction you're going, and what the connection is between the different parts of your presentation.
- Visuals allow the audience to pause, scan the message, linger for a moment, and then absorb the message more thoroughly.
- Separate ideas can be linked through such devices as acronyms. People need an organizing system to help them understand and remember.
- Research has shown that presenters using graphics are considered better prepared, more professional, more persuasive, more credible, and more interesting.

"Picture up your literature" (page 84) shows examples of how a message can be reinforced by pictures.

Picture up your literature

ARTISTS

CARTOONS

REALISTIC

ORIGINAL

NUMBERS

YOUR PERSONAL TOUCH

MOTIVATING

SIMPLICITY

Pictures by themselves are not sufficient. Although visual stimuli are capable of many things that words alone can't do, the secret is to use pictures and spoken material together. They are the two prongs in your attack. Show a picture *and* talk about it. Maximum impact will come through a carefully coordinated appeal to the two major senses — sight *and* hearing.

In Chapter 3 I explained that the fifth step in the Apple Tree Approach to session design was devising appropriate graphics — "Picture it up!" In this chapter I describe three of the most commonly used visual media — the overhead projector, flipcharts, and whiteboards — and explain how best to exploit them. There are many more visual media that might be appropriate for your presentation, such as a video recorder, movie projector, tape player, or slide projector. These media are effective in some contexts, but I have chosen not to include them in this chapter because they are not *active* visuals.

Active visuals are produced or handled by a presenter in front of the audience. They can cause a presentation to become a *two-way communication*. For example, the results of an audience survey can be recorded "live" onto a transparency by the presenter — for all to see. Active visuals do not constitute the presentation themselves, but are an effective adjunct to the spoken component. The presenter is able to maintain eye contact with the audience, constantly monitor the impact of his or her material, and adjust the delivery accordingly as the visuals are used.

OVERHEAD PROJECTORS

The most effective visual you can use is the overhead projector. Seven years ago I laughed at a professional presenter using this piece of equipment. "I don't need such toys," I said to myself. "What happens if I'm out in Birdsville doing a presentation and my bulb blows? No, not for me." Then I started working with a management consultant, Rex Ward. Sitting there in the back row of the workshop I could see the audience's interest pick up when he hit them with a picture. I watched with interest the way he used the overhead to illustrate his point, reproducing his ideas on the screen so that his audience was both seeing and hearing. Then he would ask them to do something, so that his material was being constantly reinforced.

So for me it was out with the old and in with the new. I asked Rex to show me how to use the overhead projector and design transparencies. Now, of course, I seldom work without them. In fact, on major presentations I use two overhead projectors at once.

The applications of overhead projectors

An overhead projector can be used to:

- introduce or summarize material — you can show your agenda to the audience before you begin and recap the main points at the end of your presentation
- emphasize key words — large lettering and appealing pictures allow you to strongly emphasize your main concepts
- illustrate a case study
- display a sequence — this could involve the steps in a process, for example, the handling of milk from farm to consumer, or it could involve the development of related ideas
- provide visual cues — by re-presenting a picture you have used earlier in your presentation, you provide a powerful aid to memory.

Advantages of overhead projectors

There are many advantages in using overhead projectors and few disadvantages. If you prepare your transparencies well, and anticipate mishaps, then you can overcome the few disadvantages (such as bulbs blowing and loss of focus). The advantages of an overhead projector are:

- It gives you high visual impact with both small and large groups.
- It allows you to keep eye contact with the audience while using the projector.
- It gives you effective control over timing and sequencing of your visuals.
- It allows you to stay organized with a minimum of scripting (by writing keywords on transparency borders — which are not seen by the audience).

- It is inexpensive. Overhead projectors range upward from about $700. Secondhand ones are available for around $200. Overhead projectors can also be hired from resource companies such as 3M, Bell and Howell, and Kodak.
- It is easy to operate. The on/off switch and focus are the only controls.
- It is easily transported as it is light and reasonably compact. Some brands fold down to briefcase-sized units for easy carrying.
- Transparencies are easy to produce.

Preparing transparencies

Remember the following when preparing your transparencies:
- Keep them simple.
- Use keywords, phrases, and numbers.
- Use large lettering so they can be seen from the back of the room.
- Bring them alive with color, cartoons, and pictures.
- Sketch a draft before the final production.
- Use a border within the frame — it looks good.
- Split the frame into more than one section — it makes step-by-step revelation easy.
- Make sure they say exactly what you mean.

Preparing to use the overhead projector

When you set up your room, remember that every room is different and every piece of equipment is different. You need to familiarize yourself with the actual equipment you will use and with the room before you go on.

I've developed a checklist to make sure I don't overlook anything before the presentation begins:
- Check that the overhead projector and the screen are in good working order.
- Ensure that the screen can be seen from every part of the room. A long narrow table is ideal for the projector and other material.
- Focus the projector.
- Place a watch on the table next to the projector so that I'm in control of the time.
- Place the prepared transparencies in one stack.
- Place the blank transparencies in a second stack.
- Have the handouts in a third stack.

Helpful hints on using an overhead projector

Here are 10 ideas that may help you:

- Before the presentation make sure people in the back row can *see* the screen. When you use it don't stand in front of it.

- Don't point with your finger — use a pencil. Simply place the pencil on the screen of the overhead projector and it becomes your pointer.

- Don't allow the unit to go out of focus.

- Don't leave the transparency on all the time — use it as a stimulator. Once you have finished with an idea — turn it off.

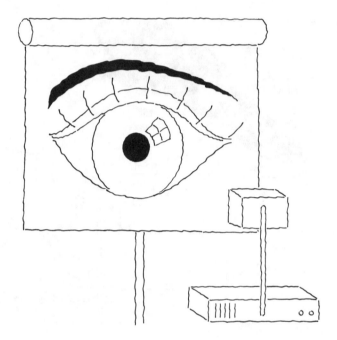

- Don't have the room so dark that the audience can't *see* you. One of the major advantages of this equipment is that it can be used in daylight.

- Don't become too casual and start talking to the screen or turn your back on the audience. Keep up the pace of the presentation.

- Why not use two overhead projectors — one for your main agenda and the other for details of your subpoints? It only takes a bit of practice to learn any new skill.

- Use overlays to add dimension and progression to your message. You can use up to four transparencies on the projector at one time.
- Use the revelation technique. Rather than exposing all your information at one time, expose only the part of the transparency you're actually talking about at that moment. Have a sheet of paper over the transparency and slide the paper down the transparency to reveal the information one line at a time.
- Use pens to highlight prepared transparencies and actually fill in the blanks while you're talking. This technique is particularly useful when you're brainstorming ideas or seeking audience involvement.

FLIPCHARTS

Flipcharts are another active and effective visual. They can be prepared ahead of time or created "live" during the function. All you need is paper, some wide-point felt-tip markers of different colors, and an easel. The new folding aluminum easels with adjustable legs are portable, convenient, and really add quality to your presentation. Use clips to hold the paper in the easel if special holes aren't built-in.

The applications of flipcharts

A flipchart can be used to:
- record and present information and ideas during presentations
- outline and reinforce key points
- present illustrations, sketches, graphs, diagrams, and other visuals.

Advantages and disadvantages of flipcharts

The advantages of flipcharts:
- They are *portable* — the paper and frame are light and easily carried.
- They are *inexpensive* — both the frame and the paper are inexpensive and easily obtained; a good quality folding aluminum easel costs about $200.
- They are a *spontaneous and flexible medium* — you can vary the way you use the flipchart according to the way the audience reacts.
- An informal atmosphere is easy to maintain when using flipcharts. The group can feel a sense of relaxed involvement with the presentation.

The disadvantages of flipcharts:
- They are not suitable for large audiences.
- Re-used charts quickly lose their freshness and begin to look old and worn.

Helpful hints on preparing a flipchart

- It is more eye-catching to include as many visuals as possible. The use of words only is likely to turn the audience off. Arouse interest with sketches, graphs, numbers, pictures, etc.
- Limit the amount of information on each page — you want to show only what you are referring to in your talk. Also a page crowded with information will be more difficult to read. Keyword your message limiting it to five words per line, and about six lines of lettering per page.
- The lettering must be large enough to be easily read from the back of the room.
- Use maximum contrast between lettering and background. Black on white is the most obvious but others, for example, black on yellow, orange on blue, green on white, are just as effective. Avoid using low contrast colors, such as pale yellow on white, or light blue on dark blue.
- Plan the layout of your prepared charts by doing a draft copy first. Keep revising your drafts until you achieve the best balance of lettering and visuals in the simplest and most eye-catching way. Then pencil your material onto the flipchart. If you don't have pre-lined paper you should lightly pencil in guidelines to ensure uniform letter size. Finish the work by going over the lines with ink, crayon, felt-tipped pen, or paint.

Helpful hints on using a flipchart

- Stand to the side of the flipchart so it is always visible to the audience and so you are always facing them when speaking.
- Place a blank sheet between each prepared page. This removes the stimulus when you've finished with it and prevents pen marks coming through on to the next prepared page.
- Write clearly and quickly when creating "live" charts.
- Turn the pages smoothly with minimum distraction.
- Have the easel high enough for everyone to see (use only the top part of the chart if necessary).
- Place tabs on the side of charts you want to refer to again in your talk.
- Lightly pencil in any notes for yourself — this cuts down on formal scripting.
- Don't reveal a chart until you are ready for it. This gives the impression of poor organization, as does showing a visual after the fact.
- Don't remain silent while you present a flipchart.

WHITEBOARDS

Another active visual that can be used either by itself, or in conjunction with the flipchart, is the whiteboard. All the equipment you need is the whiteboard itself (attached to a wall or standing on an easel), marker pens, and a cloth for erasing.

The whiteboards used for seminars and presentations vary from flipchart size to the traditional schoolroom chalkboard size.

Advantages and disadvantages of whiteboards

The advantages of whiteboards:
- Many trainers and teachers use the whiteboard to avoid the noise and mess caused by chalk and a blackboard. This is especially important if there is audiovisual equipment nearby.
- Most whiteboards are produced with a metallic backing that will enable you to attach charts, lettering, or diagrams to the board using magnetic strips.
- They provide an emergency screen for overhead projectors.

The disadvantages of whiteboards:
- The writing can be smudged easily.
- The shiny surface can give off a glare in certain lighting conditions.

Helpful hints on using a whiteboard

When using the whiteboard you should keep in mind most of the hints relating to the use of the flipchart, namely:
- Stand to the side of the board once you've finished writing on it so the audience can see it clearly.
- Never talk to the board — always look at the audience when you speak.
- Write clearly and quickly.
- Ensure the board can be seen from all parts of the room.
- Use large keywords — don't clutter the board with masses of fine print.
- Beforehand, practice the way you're going to lay out the board. Think of visibility, letter size, pictures, and writing simplicity.

REMEMBER:
- By the imaginative use of "active" visual media, you'll allow your participants to "see" what you mean — and enjoy it at the same time.
- Practice makes perfect. Practice your presentation using your visual media beforehand and you will increase your chances of a successful presentation.

7

HANDOUTS

As a professional convention goer, let me assure you of one important fact about convention people — they will kill for a handout. And once they get it, they will make a decision about you even before they see you. So the message is: *your handouts are selling*.

I was first impressed by this fact at a convention run by the American Society for Training and Development. There were more than 6,000 delegates. I witnessed a veritable stampede as normally mild-mannered delegates jostled to scoop up the handouts. No one wanted to miss out on any of the supposedly vital information, even the layout-of-the building information sheets that showed the whereabouts of the toilets.

Handouts, though, are more than just a pretty page to keep the audience happy. If designed and used effectively, they are a potent marketing tool. Apart from satisfying the participant's expectation for something to hold, read, and take home, handouts have a number of significant advantages:

- They reinforce your message by re-presenting the main points in an easy-to-read way.
- They allow you to present background material (before your talk) and additional reading (after the presentation).
- They act as a memory aid during the talk. By referring to a handout relating to an earlier part of your talk, you can make it easier for the audience to recall these points.
- By using handouts that participants fill in during your talk you encourage them to participate actively in the session. Fill-in handouts also introduce variety into your session.
- Handouts, like any well-presented visuals, bring humor and interest to your session. They have entertainment value, which you can exploit.

DESIGN AND USE OF HANDOUTS

Like any visual aid, handouts need careful planning for maximum impact. Handouts:
- must be simple
- must be directly related to the purpose of your talk
- must have high visual impact
- must not distract the audience.

Keep it simple

This applies particularly to handouts that you refer to during your talk. Use large keywords to focus attention. Learning to work with keywords helps to develop quick and easy-to-use one-line statements — they crystallize thinking and allow reading at a glance.

Have a look at the handout, "Four ingredients for effective team management" (page 98).

Four ingredients for effective team management

1 Write a daily "to do" list.

2 Set priorities for each item.

3 Schedule activities.

4 Stick to it (be ruthless).

The keywords in this handout communicate all the information in just a few words. Only the "must knows" are included — all the padding is left out.

Numbering, a form of keywording, acts as a signpost for the readers' easy reference. The illustrations express the message in pictorial and symbolic form, and entertain at the same time. There is plenty of space available for notes to be made.

Relate the handout to your talk

Your handouts are only useful if they re-present your main points. Relevance is essential.

What your audience reads must be what they hear — unless you intend to use the element of surprise. Use the same points in the same order in both your handouts and your talk. The same applies if you're using overhead transparencies.

All aspects of your presentation must be coordinated. No new material will enter the listeners' heads until they have absorbed earlier material. Let's say you've just prepared a handout which makes *Gone With The Wind* look like a short story. You hand it out just as you start your presentation. The participants scan it, prejudge it, and get bored waiting for you to catch up. Or worse still, they make paper planes out of it.

So your options are to either tidy up the handout so it easily matches up with your talk or use quality paper for the planes.

A fill-in type handout can be a good example of how closely related a handout is to the talk. On page 100 is an example of a fill-in type handout on the theme, "Improving your projected image." The participants receive the blank handout and are encouraged to fill in the information during the talk. The handout tests and re-presents the information supplied.

IMPROVING YOUR PROJECTED IMAGE — *blank handout*

There is no

How we see self
S
I

How others see us
P
I

3 ways to observe

1	**L** ....
2	**A** ....
3	**B** ....

	SOCIAL	DO YOU AGREE
1 2 3 5 4		Yes No

	BUSINESS	DO YOU AGREE
1 2 3 5 4		Yes No

IMPROVING YOUR PROJECTED IMAGE — *completed handout*

> There is no *2nd chance at a 1st impression*

How we see self	**How others see us**
S*elf*	**P***rojected*
I*mage*	**I***mage*

3 ways to observe

1	**L***anguage* ....
2	**A***ppearance* ....
3	**B***ehavior* ....

SOCIAL	DO YOU AGREE		BUSINESS	DO YOU AGREE
Attention	Yes No		*Information*	Yes No
Friendly			*Helpfulness*	
Positive			*Competence*	
Need to identify			*Trust*	

Ensure that your handout has high visual impact

With suitable art work, any material can be presented effectively in a handout.

Try reading through this list of "Twenty-one great ideas for a successful career":

1. Is this what you want?

2. Your attitude to:

   You

   Company

   Products

3. Know the nuts and bolts of the business.

4. Increase your personal association with top performers.

5. Become the number one communicator in your office.

6. Contact three prospects a day.

7. Contact three past buyers a day.

8. Cultivate contacts.

9. Prepare a "to do" list each day.

10. Set small goals.

11. Get organized.

12. Watch your:
    - language
    - appearance
    - behavior
13. Stick to the system.
14. Put the rubber on the road, not on the carpet.
15. Stay committed. P + P = P + P.
16. Set your selling quota.
17. Work with decision makers exclusively.
18. Stay in control of your emotions.
19. Take time off.
20. Stay positive.
21. Never ever stop learning.

The ideas may be useful, but the presentation is definitely at the boring end of the scale.

Now look at the same material presented with illustrations to catch the eye, set out in accessible blocks of information, and with space provided for notes (pages 104-109).

21
GREAT
IDEAS

FOR A SUCCESSFUL CAREER

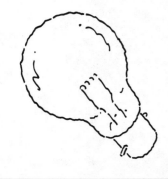

Is this what
you want?

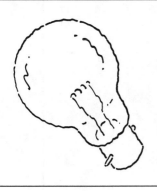

Your attitude to:
You

Company

Products

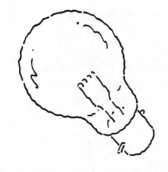

Know the nuts and
bolts of the business.

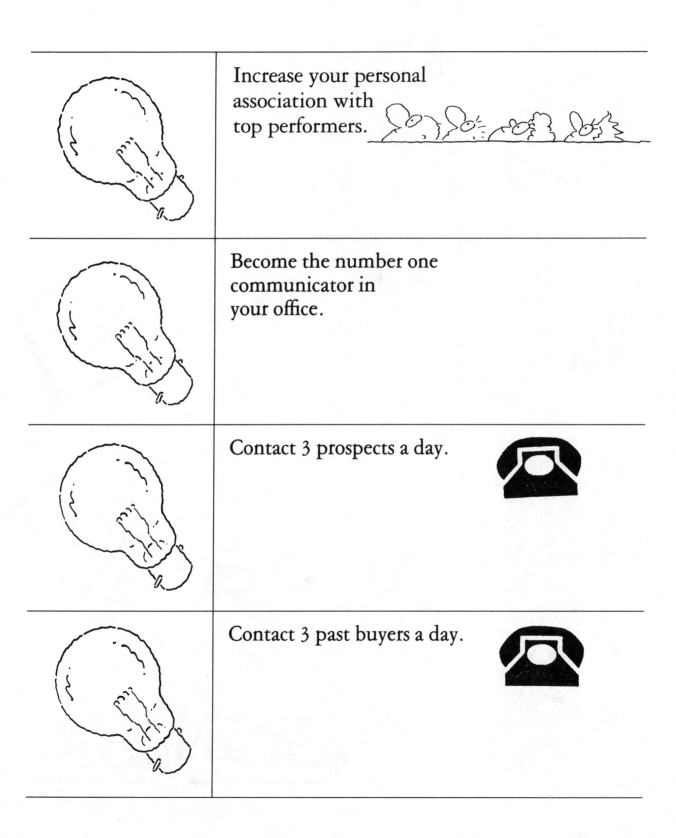

Increase your personal association with top performers.

Become the number one communicator in your office.

Contact 3 prospects a day.

Contact 3 past buyers a day.

Cultivate contacts.

Prepare a "to do" list each day.

Set small goals.

Get organized.

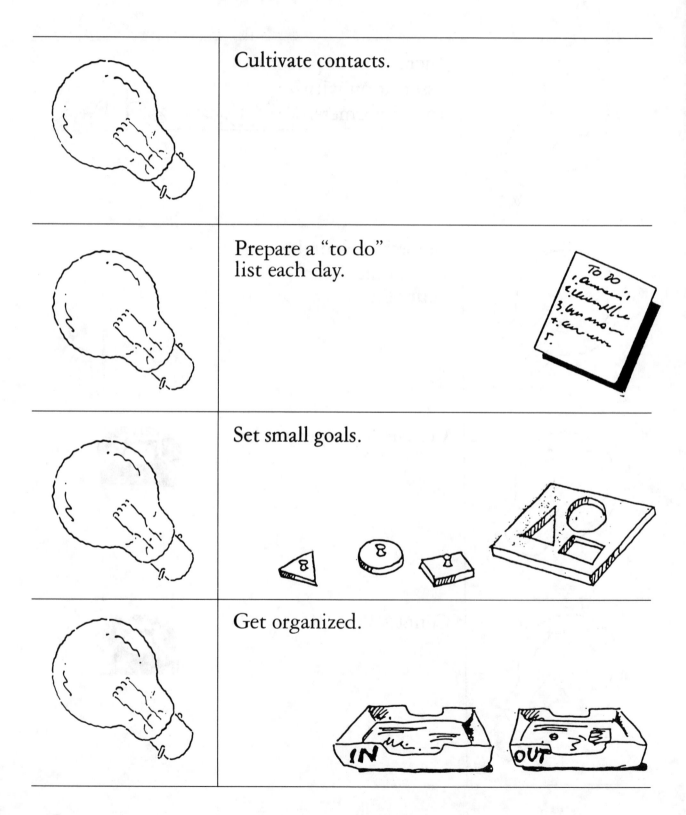

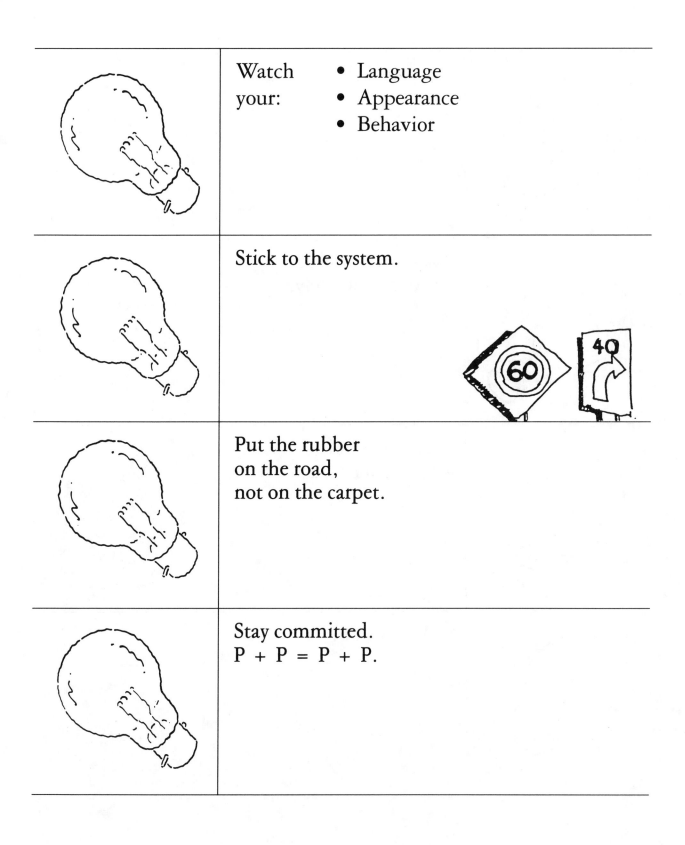

	Watch your: • Language • Appearance • Behavior
	Stick to the system.
	Put the rubber on the road, not on the carpet.
	Stay committed. P + P = P + P.

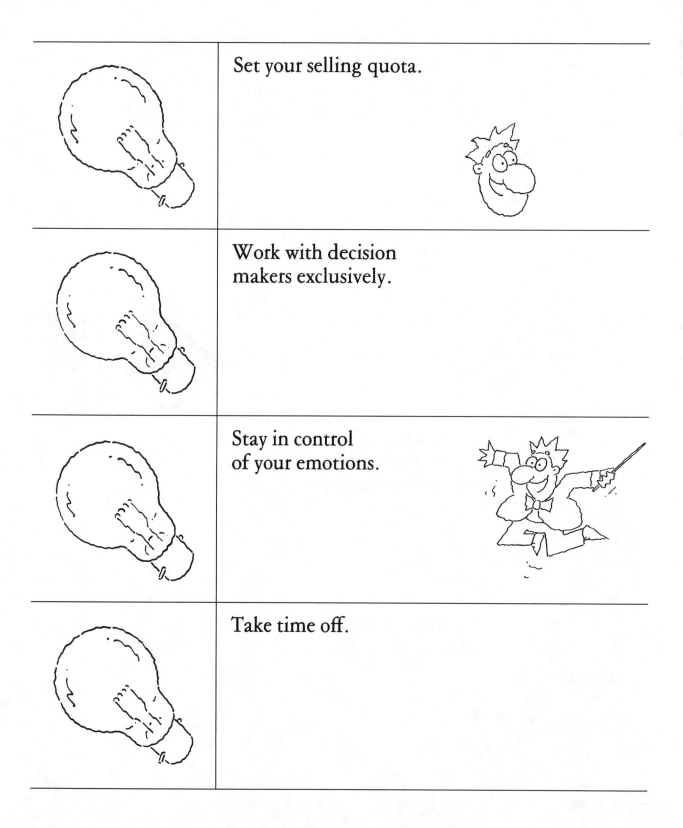

Set your selling quota.

Work with decision
makers exclusively.

Stay in control
of your emotions.

Take time off.

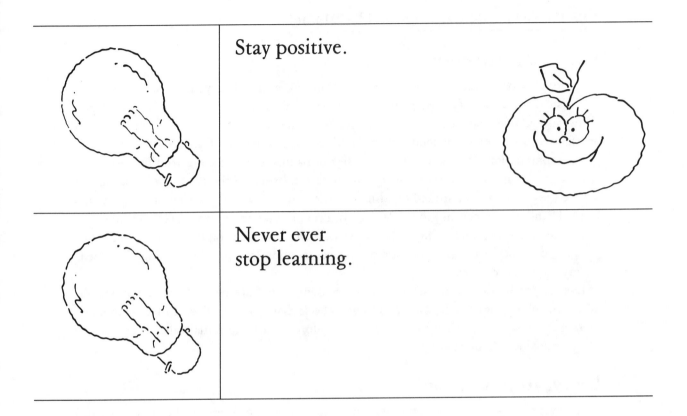

Stay positive.

Never ever
stop learning.

Ensure that your handout does not distract the audience

A handout that is not working for you will actually be working *against* you.

Handouts can distract an audience for a number of reasons. The audience will be distracted if your handout is too complicated, badly coordinated with your talk, or irrelevant to the talk. If it's too complicated in its layout or information, then it's working against you. People can only concentrate effectively on one line of thought at a time. Providing the participants with something to read that doesn't match the content of your talk only means that they will cut themselves off from one to concentrate on the other.

While it is true that there is no such thing as a boring subject, it is also true that a handout can be made more interesting than the talk. A handout can "steal" attention away from the talk. Perhaps the artist is more talented than the presenter. The handout must accurately represent the content and spirit of the talk.

DISTRIBUTION OF YOUR HANDOUT

Before the presentation

A thoroughly organized distribution means thinking ahead. Use your client checklist to establish the number of participants attending and then add 10 percent. If you're travelling, always take your master copy with you — some clients prefer to copy your material on their own premises. Handouts to be used at the beginning of your talk, or as background information, can be placed on each seat or handed out at the registration desk.

A successful method of distributing handouts and breaking the ice at the same time is for the presenter to walk around handing out the material, making welcoming comments like, "Thank you for coming today. Would you care to take these handouts?" and so on.

If your handouts involve the audience writing in some way you'll have to think about pens — but not flick-tops! You don't want several hundred people clicking their pens during your talk, do you?

During the housekeeping section of the presentation I always say, "Now you should have two yellow copies with you. Would you check that, please?" Then I give them a few moments to check that they have everything before I start the actual talk. That way, no one gets anxious about missing out.

During the presentation

If you want to "stage" your handouts, you'll need resource people to help. You should place these people in the aisle seats throughout the room, and on your instruction they hand out the material in the batches you specify. Color-coding makes this easy for the presenter, the distributors, and the participants. Joel Weldon, one of the top presenters in the field, actually counts the number of seats in each row, counts the number of handouts per row, then cross-folds them so that his resource people have the exact number of handouts for each segment of the presentation.

After the presentation

Provide extra copies for those who want them. Your master copy could be useful at this stage to run off those extra copies.

REMEMBER:
- If handouts are well-used, they significantly increase the impact of your message. They can be a powerful tool of reinforcement.
- If handouts are done badly, they will detract from your session and you will have missed out on an excellent opportunity.
- Always keep in mind the great potential of handouts, take them seriously, and you'll magnify your impact.

8

THE 10 MAJOR MISTAKES SPEAKERS MAKE

In this chapter I discuss the 10 major mistakes that speakers make when giving a presentation, with some hints on how to avoid these mistakes. This chapter also reinforces the advice of earlier chapters.

The 10 major mistakes are:
1. failing to speak to time
2. material that is not suited to the audience
3. information overload
4. material that is too technical
5. poor preparation
6. failure to practice speech
7. distracting visuals/verbals/vocals
8. inappropriate pace
9. lack of eye contact
10. lack of enthusiasm

FAILING TO SPEAK TO TIME

Once we actually start speaking, we sometimes forget to stop. We become caught up in the act of speaking and in the occasion — and we lose track of time.

Specify the length of your talk

You chose or were invited to talk on the subject — but did anyone set a time limit? As the speaker, it's usually up to you to specify the length of your talk in advance. Once you've established how long it's going to be, stick to that limit.

There are commonly accepted guidelines for the length of a talk:

- Introduction of guest speaker/vote of thanks — 3 minutes maximum
- Guest speaker to group — 20-30 minutes
- Information session/lecture — 60 minutes maximum

Make sure you stay on time

Once you've worked out the length of your talk, you need to make sure you stay on time. This can be done by:

- using a watch or clock — glance at it now and again, but don't keep looking at it
- having a friend in the audience who gives you signals
- having times for each part of your talk written on your notes — and keeping to those times.

Most of all: be time conscious. Keep in mind constantly how long you have, and try to stick to that time.

MATERIAL THAT IS NOT SUITED TO THE AUDIENCE

Don't wait until you're standing up in front of the audience to find out they're not interested in your subject. Find out before the event.

Ask three questions before you accept any speaking engagement:

1. Will they be interested in my subject?
2. Can my subject offer them any information they can use?
3. Am I the best person for the job?

To find out the answers to these questions you will have to do some homework and contact at least three members of your potential audience.

Perhaps you'll find they're not interested in your subject. If that's the case, send in another speaker.

You can't be all things to all people.

INFORMATION OVERLOAD

In our enthusiasm to let the audience know everything we know, we can overload them with too much information. There's no point swamping your audience with an avalanche of facts — they can't take it in.

- You have to be selective in what you say. Limit the amount of information to what is appropriate for the length of your talk and the abilities of your audience. Three major items in 20 minutes is enough for most people to handle. It's better for your audience to remember three facts well, than for them to quickly forget a dozen facts.
- Present your information in bite-size pieces, just enough for your audience to take in once at a time.
- Relate your information to everyday experiences. That will make it easy for your audience to understand its importance, and to remember it.
- Reinforcement is essential. Tell them what you will tell them. Tell them the same thing in a different way. Tell them again using a parallel.

To communicate effectively you must make it easy for your audience to remember what you're saying.

MATERIAL THAT IS TOO TECHNICAL

Recently I was having a discussion with a friend of mine who is a computer programmer. He was trying to explain to me what the problem was with our office computer. But I couldn't follow his explanation because he was using technical language, such as cursor, link-bin files, etc. So I asked him to translate what he was saying into non-technical language. He went further than that — he drew out the problem in cartoons and showed me the solution *in my terms.*

Every industry has its own jargon, but unless you are talking to a group from your own industry, *don't use jargon.* They won't be able to follow you.

- Translate your talk into a level of language that is appropriate for your audience.
- Relate your information to experiences that they are likely to have, and then they'll understand it.

Put another way, you need to "transmit on their frequency" for them to take in your talk.

POOR PREPARATION

"The truth behind every spectacular presentation is heaps of unspectacular preparation."

You might be one of the lucky few who can go unprepared and do well, but if you're not, then heed this advice of Dr. Ken McFarlane and go through the process of researching, planning, and drafting your material.

- Start with a *brainstorm,* a spontaneous ideas session, where you jot down everything that comes into your head to do with the subject.
- *Keyword* this material, that is, select a few words that are focus or keywords, and then build on them.
- *Reinforce* your key topics with personal stories, analogies, references to the intended audience's own experience, and visual aids.

This is essentially what the Apple Tree Approach to session design is about.

Detailed, thorough preparation leads to effective presentation.

FAILURE TO PRACTICE SPEECH

Giving a presentation is a skill that you can develop. Like the improvement of any skill it needs a *program of practice*.

Consider the case of a fellow called Rick. Rick is an accomplished guitar player and he performs at major concerts all over the country.

Rick signed up for one of my public speaking classes. After night one he came up to me and said, "Doug, I don't get it. Here I am at 27, a guitarist performing in front of up to 5,000 people at a time...and doing it well. But tonight in front of 10 people my nerves are a mess. What's wrong with me tonight?" I started by asking him to calculate how many times he'd practiced his guitar playing since he began his career. "Three time a day every day for the last 10 years, down in the garage," he replied.

I continued, "Every time you get up on stage to play in front of an audience you're going through a routine that you've practiced thousands of times! Now, public speaking is just the same. It's a skill that you or I or anyone can learn through practice. If you learn to control your reactions under simulated conditions, you'll have a much better chance of controlling them under real conditions."

I suggested he try the three tests I found so useful when I first started:

- the *spot* test
- the *paper* test
- the *music* test

The spot test

I call it the spot test because it involves focusing on a spot on the wall as you rehearse your talk.

Here's what to do: In your imagination set the scene for your speech — the hall, the audience, the time, etc. Then visualize the lead up to your talk — the introduction.

Then, stand up and start, "Good evening, thank you for inviting me..." and say it with *conviction* as if it really were the big event. As you go through your speech, focus on a spot on the wall. The reason for this is that if you can't talk in front of a blank wall, you won't be able to talk in front of people. And if you feel self-conscious, remember — all the best public speakers (as well as actors, politicians, and performers of any sort) have done it at some stage — and no one will know anyway.

The paper test

This activity trains you to keep your feet still while you speak. Place a piece of ordinary white paper on the floor. Stand on it, and then draw around your shoes with a felt-tip pen — and that's where your feet have to stay while you speak.

Now go through the spot test again, keeping your feet under control as you speak.

The music test

Our guitarist, Rick, thought he'd like this one. At a speaking engagement there are many distractions — noises from outside, people coming and going. Once you allow yourself to he distracted, you lose your train of thought.

To prevent this from happening to you try the music test. Put on some music with the volume set just above comfortable listening level. Start your talk with the music playing, focusing on the spot, and keeping your feet still.

At first you'll find it almost impossible to maintain your line of thought. But you'll get better at it, and you'll be able to concentrate on what counts — getting your message across in a fun and exciting way.

Rick could see the sense in these suggestions and headed off for his first practice session in his garage.

So find your own garage and put in some practice, controlling your reactions under simulated conditions.

DISTRACTING VISUALS/VERBALS/VOCALS

There are three aspects of a presentation that influence the effectiveness of your communication:
- visual aspect — what they see you do
- verbal aspect — what they hear you say
- vocal aspect — how they hear you say it

All of these work together to make your message clear and interesting.

The most powerful effect is visual — facial expression, gestures, body stance — and if there is any competition among the three, the visual will predominate.

Learn to control any distracting habits you may have that affect the visual, verbal, and vocal aspects of your presentation. Ask a friend to tell you of any distracting habits you display while speaking, habits such as standing on one foot, scratching your nose, using "um," "ah," "you know," "sort of," or a slurred, unclear, or monotonous way of speaking.

Use an audio or video recorder to allow you to analyze your voice or picture.

Pinpoint any problems and then eliminate them so that the visual, verbal, and vocal aspects of your presentation reinforce each other.

INAPPROPRIATE PACE

Your audience needs time to take in what you're saying. Speaking more quickly than they can take it in means your message is being lost. Sixty to seventy words per minute is fast enough.

Delivering an effective speech is like driving a car — you need to speed up and slow down now and again, but mostly you move along at a steady pace.

When you are talking you vary the pace to reinforce your message.

- Practice with a metronome. The regular beat will help you pace your delivery.
- Use a cassette recorder to check your rate.
- Use the pause for effect, and to wait for laughter, noise, etc. to die down.
- Observe the audience as you speak and adjust your pace to maximize the effect on them.

The pace of your delivery should reinforce your message.

LACK OF EYE CONTACT

When you're having a conversation with another person, you look that person in the eye. That way the other person knows you're talking to him or her and maintains a direct, open contact.

It's the same with public speaking. If you establish eye contact with individual members of the audience, they will be drawn into your talk, and they will feel that you are speaking directly to each of them.

Don't look up at the ceiling, as if your cue cards are stuck up there. Look people in the eye. If you're using notes, pause each time you refer to them, then re-establish eye contact and continue your talk.

Practice in front of a mirror; or, better still, have a friend monitor your eye contact during your speech.

If you look at your audience, they will keep listening.

LACK OF ENTHUSIASM

When you're speaking in front of a group of people, you're a salesperson for your own ideas, a performer presenting a show. You're projecting your personality.

If you're enthusiastic about a subject in which you have a genuine interest, it will come across in your talk. The audience will be convinced that you believe that your subject is interesting and important. *They'll buy your ideas*.

But if you drag yourself up there and start off in a monotonous, droning voice with something like, "Tonight I'm here to talk to you about the life cycle of the earth worm," then your attitude will be catching. You'll bore them just as much as you are bored, if not more.

- First of all, don't hide behind the lectern. Let yourself be seen.
- Start off on a lively and encouraging note with something like "I am delighted to be here tonight to share my ideas with you."
- Keep up the pace, especially at the start of your talk, when judgments are being formed about you.
- Employ all your presentation skills to convey your enthusiasm — an expressive voice, appropriate gestures and emphasis, and humor.

Use the full force of your personality to project your enthusiasm for the subject.

REMEMBER:
- Be well-prepared — both for your audience and with your material.
- Practice! Practice! Practice!
- *Communicate* with your audience — maintain eye contact and speak with enthusiasm.

9

EVALUATION

Unless you make a deliberate effort, you'll never totally know how well your session went.

I use five ways of evaluating a presentation:

- resource personnel
- resource equipment
- evaluation card
- "live" evaluation
- self-evaluation

I usually use two or more of these methods for each presentation.

RESOURCE PERSONNEL

No matter what *you*, the presenter, thought about the presentation, there will be others who saw it in a different light. It's very difficult, some would say impossible, to view yourself through the eyes of another.

Resource personnel, assistants who take part in the session and closely observe you and the audience's reactions, can be very useful in the evaluation process.

When I began my career as a presenter I read all the right books, prepared myself thoroughly, and thought I knew pretty well what was going on in my presentations. Then one time an old hometown fiend of mine came along to a large presentation I was giving in Melbourne. He wanted to see how the local boy had made good in the big city. After the session, over dinner, he produced some remarkable facts about my performance that day:

- I had turned my back on a quarter of the audience during vital explanations.
- I had used the word "horrifically" 14 times.
- I had pointed with my finger on the screen of the overhead projector while explaining the rules for using the overhead projector effectively.
- I had failed to realize that a third of the audience didn't have pens to fill out one of my hot-shot participative handouts.

Threatening as this information was, I realized its truth, and learned in one rather painful lesson the benefits of objective evaluation of my performance.

Now in every major presentation, I have at least one resource person, whose job is solely to assess my performance. A resource person has the ability to consider both your performance and the audience's reaction, by moving around and helping the audience. He or she can also provide you with a critique of:

- your material
- your method of presentation
- your presentation skills (including distracting mannerisms)
- audience reaction and understanding.

RESOURCE EQUIPMENT

Both audio and video recorders allow you to hear and see exactly what went on. A sound recording on a cassette or tape recorder is obviously more limited than a video recording, but if you particularly want to assess your *spoken* presentation, then the cassette player is just what you need.

A small unit placed on your table or held by a helper near the front will be unobtrusive, and will let you know exactly *what* you (and the participants) said and, just as important, *how* you said it.

The "mirror with a memory" — the video recorder — is more complicated to set up and run, but it allows you to hear and see exactly what went on in your presentation. You'll be strongly impressed — perhaps not favorably — by the way you look the first time you see yourself on video. It's a very revealing medium, showing all the little gestures, movements, and facial expressions that you might not really want to see in yourself.

But your "private screening" will also show you what looked good and what went well, and allow you to refine the technique of your delivery.

EVALUATION CARD

I (or my resource people, depending on the numbers) hand out the "Evaluation card" (page 122) at the end of my presentation and ask the audience to fill it in. Pens are supplied for those who need them.

Evaluation card

What did you think? Feedback is necessary to any speaker. Would you please complete this form?

SCORE

What impact did the presentation have on you?

Unfavorable　　　　　　Favorable

1 2 3 4 5 6 7 8 9 10 ....

Were you impressed with the material delivered by the speaker?

No — not very　　　　　Yes — very

1 2 3 4 5 6 7 8 9 10 ....

Did you obtain any information that you can use?

No — useless　　　　　Excellent
information　　　　　　information

1 2 3 4 5 6 7 8 9 10 ....

What did you like best?

What did you like least?

Comments:

**IF YOU WOULD LIKE TO GO ON OUR MAILING LIST FOR RESOURCE MATERIAL,
PRINT YOUR NAME ON THE OTHER SIDE OF THIS CARD.**

I use this card with numbers up to about a hundred. There's too much work involved reading and collating the material with numbers much larger than a hundred. "Live" evaluation, discussed below, is more suited to larger groups.

If you score eight out of ten on any of the ratings, then you're doing well. People are very reluctant to give ten out of ten — perhaps they don't recognize perfection when they see it!

On the bottom of the card, you can see the invitation to join the resource material mailing list. There are two reasons for this offer:

- Maybe they genuinely do want to maintain contact with you — a contact that could benefit you as much as them.
- Having the respondent's name on the card lets you put a face to that name and so lets you make a judgment about his or her evaluation of you.

"LIVE" EVALUATION

There are many live evaluation techniques that you can use successfully. They all involve the audience *doing* something, either in pairs or in larger groups. Three live evaluation techniques are discussed below:

- brainstorming
- voting with your feet
- picture it up

Live evaluation techniques are best used at the end of a session where you've used a lot of audience participation. Your participants will be relaxed and willing to speak freely and cooperate effectively.

Brainstorming

Divide the audience into equal-sized groups, about 10 to a group. Provide each group with a flipchart or transparency, and markers. Nominate, or get each group to elect, a group leader who can direct the activity and be the group scribe. The "brainstorming" session now begins.

Each member is encouraged to express comments on the positive and negative aspects of the presentation. The group leader records the comments as keywords or phrases on the flipchart or transparency.

As presenter, you might choose to limit the categories they are to discuss, or you might leave it completely open, depending on the abilities of the group.

Set a time limit in advance for the activity and explain that the results will be presented to the whole audience at the end of the activity. One of your resource people can then tabulate the results.

Voting with your feet

This technique also works well with a group that has participated enthusiastically.

Explain to everyone that they are going to "vote with their feet," i.e., go and stand in one of three parts of the room which indicate how much they learned in the session:

- high level of learning
- moderate level of learning
- low level of learning

Then ask one or two members from each group to explain to the whole group why they are standing in that area. Have your resource person keyword the comments onto an overhead projector or flipchart for all to see.

Picture it up

For a group that's been through a session where the emphasis was on high visual input, this technique can be very successful.

Provide transparencies and projectors, flipcharts, markers, rolls of paper, and adhesive, whatever you can think of that allows the production of vibrant visuals. Explain to the whole group that singly or in groups of their choosing they are going to produce *visual* evaluations of the session — sketches, diagrams, graphs, cartoons, symbols, flowcharts.

You could allocate time for this procedure frequently through the session to promote a sense of sequence and skill acquisition. Participants are then encouraged to walk around the room and comment on the work of the others.

Considerations in using live techniques

Audience members at a presentation, as with most groups of people, *like* to be asked what they think. Evaluation to this extent is an end in itself. It gives people the opportunity to let off a bit of steam, or at least to feel they have some control over the proceedings. So appease them, let them tell you what they think. If things did go wrong, it's better they complain in the session, rather than back in the office.

Live evaluations can be quite intimidating for the presenter. Some people don't pull any punches at all — they'll tell you exactly what they disliked about your presentation. So be prepared to grin and bear it. Avoid live evaluation if there's obvious hostility that could introduce bad feeling into the session. You want to encourage constructive criticisms and discourage destructive comments.

You'll find that most of the negative observations tend to be about the environment — too stuffy, uncomfortable seating, or distracting noise. Usually you won't have any control over these aspects, and that's your best reply.

Live evaluation techniques tend to promote group cohesion — everyone ends up knowing what everyone else thinks. If you're into effective communication, what better way to finish!

SELF-EVALUATION

"If I had to do it again, what would I do differently?" Ask yourself that after each presentation. Consider what you've *said*, *shown*, and *done*.

I've spoken on some topics over a dozen times. The speeches are never exactly the same, though, I'm pleased to say. By evaluating my own performance I've managed to improve my delivery greatly. The more you do it, the fewer are the changes, but there still are minor improvements possible in any presentation.

Be constructive with yourself. Express changes as "alternative positive behaviors." ("That example was okay, but next time I'll use another example that brings out the point more clearly.")

REMEMBER:
- If your aim is to improve your skills as a presenter, evaluation of your presentation is essential.
- Evaluation may be a little damaging to the ego, but the satisfaction of doing better next time compensates for any damage.
- With appropriate evaluation techniques, fine-tuning of your performance will become second nature. There's always room, no matter how small, for improvement!

IS THIS THE END?

No, this is not the end; this is the *beginning — the beginning of a new and exciting period in your life as a presenter.* Next time you dress yourself up and head off for some personal growth and sit in a classroom or attend a convention, do not observe the speaker, observe the audience. Are they alive or dead?

Then say to yourself — If I were the presenter what could I have done or what could I have said that would make the audience come alive?

As a professional student, I attend everything that opens and shuts and I have learned that the dynamic, exciting, fun presenters are remembered. The other lesson I have learned is that they are in the minority. In fact my own unofficial research would suggest that about one in ten people actually presents effectively. Mind you, the other nine think they do.

You and I are responsible for the outcome. No subject is boring; there are only boring speakers. So stay alive, present well, and learn to give top performances. If you do this, your career as a presenter will grow and you will become a sought-after speaker.

I hope you have enjoyed participating with me through this book and I look forward to hearing from you, suggesting that these ideas actually did work for you when it was your time to stand up and speak.

Answer to 'Squares Quiz'

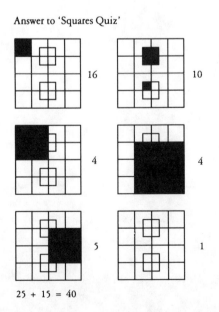

25 + 15 = 40

RECOMMENDED READING LIST

BRAUDE, J. M. *Braude's Treasury of Wit and Humour*. Prentice-Hall Inc., Englewood Cliffs, New Jersey, 1964

HIGBEE, K. L. *Your Memory — How it Works and How to Improve It*. Prentice-Hall Inc., Englewood Cliffs, New Jersey, 1977

LEECH, T. *How to Prepare, Stage And Deliver Winning Presentations*. AMACOM, New York, 1982

LITVAK, S. and SENZEE A. W. *More Ways to Use Your Head*. Prentice-Hall Inc., Englewood Cliffs, New Jersey, 1985

MALOUF, D. *Confidence Through Public Speaking*. Information Australia, Melbourne, 1983

PENDLETON, W. K. *Speaker's Handbook of Successful Openers and Closers*. Prentice-Hall Inc., Englewood Cliffs, New Jersey, 1984

SCANNELL, E. E. and NEWSTROM, J. W. *Games Trainers Play*. McGraw-Hill Book Company, New York, 1983

SCANNELL, E. E. and NEWSTROM, J. W. *More Games Trainers Play*. McGraw-Hill Book Company, New York, 1983

VECCHIET, D. and HAZELL, H. *A Drop of Ink to Make Millions Think*. Ian Coles Publishing, Sydney, 1983

WILLIAMS, L. V. *Teaching for the Two-sided Mind*. Prentice-Hall Inc., Englewood Cliffs, New Jersey, 1983

WITT, S. *How to be Twice as Smart*. Parker Publishing Company Inc., West Nyack, New York, 1983

YEOMANS, W. N. *1000 Things You Never Learned in Business School*. McGraw-Hill Book Company, New York, 1985

INDEX